# mum
## ultrapreneur

# mum
## ultrapreneur

susan ödev
mark weeks

First Published In Great Britain 2010
by www.BookShaker.com

© Copyright Susan Ödev & Mark Weeks

All rights reserved. No part of this publication may be reproduced, stored in or introduced into a retrieval system, or transmitted, in any form, or by any means (electronic, mechanical, photocopying recording or otherwise) without the prior written permission of the publisher.

This book is sold subject to the condition that it shall not, by way of trade or otherwise, be lent, resold, hired out, or otherwise circulated without the publisher's prior consent in any form of binding or cover other than that in which it is published and without a similar condition including this condition being imposed on the subsequent purchaser.

Typeset in Bookman Old Style

*Dedicated to amazing mums all
over the world who 'just do it'*

# Contents

**CONTENTS**

**HUGE THANKS**

**PRAISE**

**FOREWORD** ............................................................... 1

**INTRODUCTION** ....................................................... 3

## PART ONE

**WHY MUM ULTRAPRENEUR?** ................................. 7
    Are You A Mum Ultrapreneur? ................................... 8
    Susan's View: The Birds & The Bees! ....................... 12
    Mark's View: There's Always A Way ......................... 17

**GROWING FAMILY, GROWING BUSINESS, GROWING STRONGER** ............................................................. 26

## PART TWO

**GEMMA'S STORY** ................................................... 31
    1: Keep it simple ~~stupid~~ ... sexy! ................................. 31
    2: Eureka! ..................................................................... 42
    3. One small Step For Woman, But One Giant Leap For (Man)kind! ........................................................... 58
    4: Mamma Mia! ............................................................ 67
    5: Let It Be .................................................................... 75
    6: A Chocolate & Duvet Day! ..................................... 84
    7: Fake It Till You Make It! ........................................... 96
    8: Don't Look Back in Anger ..................................... 104

## PART THREE

## MEET THE MUM ULTRAPRENEURS ..................... 119

    S is for Simplicity ............................................... 120
    P is for Passion .................................................. 131
    A is for Action ................................................... 138
    R is for Relationships ......................................... 147
    K is for Knowing ................................................ 157
    L is for Learning ................................................ 164
    E is for Enthusiasm ............................................ 172
    S is for Self Belief ............................................... 180
    Case Study ........................................................ 191

## A MOTHER'S WISDOM ........................................ 195

## PART FOUR

## THE SPARKLES PLAN ......................................... 205

    Part A: The Big Idea ........................................... 206
    Part B: Making It Happen ................................... 210
    Simplicity ............................................................ 210
    Passion ............................................................... 213
    Action ................................................................ 213
    Relationships ..................................................... 215
    Knowing ............................................................ 217
    Learning ............................................................ 218
    Enthusiasm ........................................................ 219
    Self-belief .......................................................... 221

## WELL DONE! ...................................................... 222

## MUM ULTRAPRENEUR READING LIST ............... 225

    References ......................................................... 229

# Huge Thanks

Firstly there are some people we both want to thank for all their help and support.

We have to start with the Mumpreneurs, or should that be Mum Ultrapreneurs, many of you have become firm friends and without your candid wisdom, humour and insightful advice we wouldn't have a book. Listening to the interviews when editing was so inspiring and ignited within us a passion to ensure that somehow, some way, this book would see the light of day. Thank you.

And that leads us to four special people without whom the book would not have existed: our brilliant transcriber, Belinda Scott, who turned every golden nugget spoken during the interviews into the written word. Belinda, you are a star. Debbie Jenkins and Joe Gregory, our publishers at Bookshaker.com have shown unswerving faith in us and this project – you are literary geniuses. And last but not least Sylvia Howe, our editor, for removing the many bloopers and making us sound articulate!

## Susan

My personal thanks could easy fill another book. It has been an amazing journey and there are so many people who have supported and encouraged me along the way. If I have omitted you by name (you know who you are) know that I honour you in my heart and love you all.

Support via the virtual world of Facebook and Twitter has been staggering and I am sorry I just haven't got room to roll call you all here. But a special thank you goes to my 'real' world friends who never once said 'Are you mad? Who do you think you are writing a book?' so, in alphabetical order, massive thank yous to Amanda Crowter, Barbara Hainsworth, Funke

Adebusuyi, Karen Muxworthy, Lesley Hawkins and Samantha Persand.

Of course I have to thank my co-author Mark for his creativity and constant faith in me, and women generally, and to his wife and family for allowing him on the computer at all times of the day and night!

But, and it's a big but, my biggest thank you has to go to my family:

My ever-patient, ever-supportive Mum – thank you for making me the woman I am today and being there through all the hard times. I love you.

My hard working, 'scrumptious' husband Cuneyt and his excited and encouraging family back in Turkey – Nacide(Anne), Tansu, Deniz and Zeynep.

My brother Charles, an awesome business mind, his partner Serena, and his great boys: Daniel, Aaron and Joshua.

My cousin Julia – I'll never forget when I first spoke to you about this and you were so there for me and have been every day since.

My aunt Margaret, my cousins Stuart, John and Regina and all my other aunts, uncles and cousins scattered across the British Isles and beyond.

And most importantly my reasons for getting up in the morning and wanting to 'just do it!' ... my beautiful children: Aslan, Tara, Alpy and Summer. You guys are my world. I love you more than life or Lindor Chocs (and you know how much I love them!) You are my motivation and my reward.

# **Mark**

Thank you.

(The one thing Susan has drummed into me is less is more, so I should leave it there but I'm a slow learner...)

So...

...though many of you will just skip over this section and get to the heart of the book (it's okay, I do the same when reading others' acknowledgements) but being this side of the fence is different. Now I completely understand the teamwork, effort and support that goes on behind the scenes to produce a book.

And it's no coincidence that the people who have helped me the most, inspired me the most, and to whom I have turned for encouragement are mostly women.

So my biggest thank yous must go firstly to my wife Sarah and my mother for their constant love and affection and for putting up with me even when they thought I was slightly barmy at times.

And for getting me to take the much needed action in putting pen to paper I would love to thank Rachel Elnaugh, former Dragon, author and business mentor. Without her initial encouragement and belief I may not have taken that first tough step. Thank you Rachel for reading the very rough drafts and urging me to go for it.

And though I took that step it was through the efforts of my good friend Susan that those rough drafts took on form and shape. I will always be thankful for her tireless efforts in turning my snippets of creativity into a complete book - that actually made sense!

Also I have to make a special mention to Sarah Tremellen CEO of Bravissimo, for her enthusiasm in the early stages of the project and willingness to talk openly about her life. It was the uncanny resemblance of her experiences to the outline draft of Gemma's story that inspired Susan and me to explore more deeply the emotional and mental aspects of being an entrepreneur and why women naturally have so many of these qualities.

But the biggest thank you of all must go to my daughters Emma and Amelia: my inspiration and constant reminder of what is most important in this world. Love and laughter. As they are 'trainee' women, it's my life's work to ensure they know they have the options and answers within themselves to be whatever they may want to be.

Finally, a big thank you to you for taking the time to read our book... hope you enjoy it.

# Praise

*'Be inspired... be VERY inspired!'*
**Tanya Rostron, Managing Director, Water at Work (Midlands) ltd, www.wateratworkmidlands.co.uk**

*'As a Mumpreneur, I was intrigued to learn what a Mum Ultrapreneur is! I thought that this description sounded fascinating and upon further reading, discovered that the term Ultrapreneur is more holistic- not just referring to the fact that you are a mum in business. I tried to skim through the book as with my own business, 2 children, blog and writing of my own to do, I have little free time but I have to confess I was sucked in to reading the whole book- it was too interesting to put down! This book is a mini novel, self help guide and business non-fiction book rolled into one, and if you are a mum and even thinking of running a business, then Mum Ultrapreneur is a great place to start!'*
**Nadine Hill, www.TheDreamPA.co.uk**

*'There is nothing better than realizing that there can be harmony between running a successful business and raising a strong family. Susan and Mark not only demonstrate that possibility, they show you how it can be true for you!'*
**Doreen Banaszak, Author, www.excusemeyourlifeisnow.com**

*'If you are looking for inspiration, try reading Mum Ultrapreneur. I loved the central story of one, fictional, mum and how she made her life SPARKLE. In Mum Ultrapreneur you can read about Susan and Mark's method to make your life SPARKLE too.'*
**Antonia Chitty, Inspirational Business Mum of the Year 2009, www.themumpreneurguide.co.uk**

*'Mum Ultrapreneur is a must for any mum thinking or wanting to take the plunge into self-employment. I loved the juxtaposition of the fictitious character Gemma, and her journey from her initial idea and thoughts, alongside the reality of other leading and well know business mummies thoughts and struggles. The SPARKLE idea is fab! I love the simplicity of it and yet it really does get your grey matter working... I only wish I'd read this a year ago when I was starting up, however this will be the basis of my business plan from now on! Such an easy to read book I thoroughly enjoyed it.'*
          **Joanne Dewberry, www.charliemoos.co.uk**
          **and winner of Future 100 Awards 2009**

*'If it is inspiration that you are after then this book has it..bucket loads of it. It offers plenty of insight and advice from mums who have been there and done it. Use this book to propel you from inactivity to Mum Ultrapreneur!'*
          **Wendy Shand, www.totstofrance.co.uk**

# Foreword

When Susan asked me if I would write the foreword for this book without a moment's thought I said yes. What was there to think about? A book whose aim is to motivate and inspire mums to take their business ideas and 'just do it' – of course I was up for that.

I am a firm believer in the absolute fact that everyone has the ability to achieve great success in their lives if they choose to do so. It's all about attitude. Know what you want and go for it.

I met Susan at a networking event for business mums run by Alli Price, just one of the amazing mums interviewed for the this book. Over 45 women had travelled from across London and the surrounding counties to meet, enjoy a fine meal and listen to me speak. I was almost lost for words... almost. The energy in the room that lunchtime. The positive vibe. The almost tangible feeling of determination and creativity was incredible and I went home with my own head buzzing with ideas and new contacts.

I was there as a so-called expert but, to be honest, I was just like every other woman in the room. I am a mum, I am a wife and at the end of the day I still do the housework and take my control pants off one leg at a time! For all my celebrity status, since being on *The Apprentice*, *Beat the Boss* and subsequent TV and other media roles, yes I had a name but that has opened few doors for my baby skincare products *Miamoo*. In fact, just before the lunch I had received several quite major setbacks in the promotion of my *Miamoo* product line and was being forced into re-evaluating my business strategy or risk losing all that I had built up so passionately.

And that's what I believe is so fantastic about this book Mum Ultrapreneur. Susan and Mark have focused on how to take the ordinary that is within all of us and make it SPARKLE!

What I also love is the way they have approached it. In my book *P.U.S.H. For Success* I talk about learning about yourself and the importance of continuous self development. To do that you have to know what works for you. Are you a Visual or an Auditory or Touchy-feely (Kinaesthetic) learner? Your learning style will affect how you receive and process information and learning. In this book there are a variety of ways in. There are the debate and statistics sections in Part One to get your mind going and then in Part Two, for those of you who prefer to see the world in pictures, there's the fictional story of Gemma. Gemma has a lot of drive and ambition but hits some major brick walls like we all do from time to time. And, like all of us can, with the right attitude and with support from the people who love her she gets there and so can you. And if you are in any doubt Part Three is filled to breaking with the insights of over 30 incredible business mums. I know that I learnt a lot from their experiences and the great bit is, whilst many are well established in business, others are just starting out, working through the issues, just like you or I. And for those of you, like me, who want to just jump straight in and get going Part Four has a powerful and practical plan to get you started.

What are you waiting for? This is a fun read, full of humour and wisdom. So:

- Read
- Be inspired
- Prepare... and then,
- Just do it!

**Saira Khan, Director, Miamoo (www.miamoo.co.uk)**
**Star of TV's The Apprentice, presenter, columnist**
**and author of P.U.S.H. For Success**

# Introduction

This is not a self help book – it's a business proposal.

*Life is not easy for any of us. But what of that? We must have perseverance and, above all, confidence in ourselves. We must believe that we are gifted for something, and that this thing, at whatever cost, must be attained.*
Marie Curie 1867-1934

These words, written by one of the world's most remarkable women, say it all really. (Whilst Marie Curie is best remembered for her huge contribution to the fight against cancer she was also, less famously...a working mum.)

Madame Curie understood that it is a natural part of the human condition to strive to be the very best that one can be. It may not be easy but this call cannot go unanswered. It also sums up motherhood, doesn't it? At times it will seem impossible but you will find a way – you have to.

If you have picked up this book, it is likely that you too are looking for a way to be the very best that you can be and are probably a mother or mum-to-be. So we will assume that you want the very best not for you but for your family as well. But isn't 'Having It All' a myth? Surely Superwoman laid down her satin cape back in 1989?

Becoming pregnant, for the first or the fourth time, is inevitably a time for simultaneous reflection and forward planning. The act of bringing a new life into the world makes every woman consider her choices.

- Should I become a stay-at-home mum?
- Should I return to work?
- Full time or part time?
- What is best for my child(ren)?
- Can I afford the child care?
- What is the best solution for me?
- Will my mind atrophy if I stay at home?
- I love finger painting but…can we afford to lose my salary?
- Maybe…I can turn my love for finger painting into a business?

Starting or extending the family unit should be a joyous anxiety-free time but we all know that in this modern age there are no simple answers to life's complex questions…or are there?

This book was written to help you explore the choices open to you. It is our passion to help you find your passion and to point you towards further advice and guidance for taking action. We have talked to many women who have been in exactly the same situation as you.

We have been there too.

Susan is a working mum with four children ranging in age from 18 to seven. And has tried it all: returning to work full time and part time, staying at home and starting her own business.

Mark is a businessman (can't blame him for his gender). He is married with two young daughters and supports his wife Sarah unconditionally. He has, though, seen at first hand the positive and negative impact work-related decisions can have on the family unit and believes there is a better way.

The following chapters will dance with the range of options available to you. There is no right way, only your way. If, by the end of Chapter Three, you are convinced that you want to, or have to, return to work we have a list of resources to ease your transition on our website *www.mum-ultrapreneur.com*

That, however is not the main focus of this book.

There is something about setting up on your own, forming your own company, following through on your great idea or chasing your dream that has led you to this book.

And you are not alone.

There are a growing number of sisters doing it for themselves; we have talked to many of them. You will find their inspiring words of wisdom in Part Three. There are also FREE BONUS audio downloads of the interviews available at *www.mum-ultrapreneur.com/bonuses*

The best bit about interviewing these amazing women was the discovery that they are ordinary mums like you.

As you read and explore the theory, research and ideas in Part One, reflect on Gemma's fictional story in Part Two and enjoy the true stories and absorb the wisdom in Part Three ... you will discover that you too are an ordinary mum who is capable of doing amazing things. Part Four is there to help you get things started.

So, are you ready?

Then we'll begin!

**Susan and Mark**
**www.mum-ultrapreneur.com**

Susan Ödev & Mark Weeks

# Part One

# Why Mum Ultrapreneur?

*And so our mothers and grandmothers have, more often than not anonymously, handed on the creative spark, the seed of the flower they themselves never hoped to see - or like a sealed letter they could not plainly read.*
Alice Walker

**ULTRAPRENEUR** n. (pl. Ultrapreneurs (very rare))

*Radical spirit whose restless pursuit of innovative business excellence is unbounded; recognised as a super-heroic leader of hearts and minds. Engages in ultraprising.*
Peter Jones, entrepreneur, famous Dragon and father[1]

---

[1] Though he states on his website he actually coined this word in response to media mocking of his accent when he said entrepreneur.

**MUM** n. (pl. Mums alt. Mom, Mummy, Mother, Ma. Mama. Mamma, Momma, Mammy, Mater)

*Amazing woman who gives birth to, adopts or takes on the female parenting role to one or more child. Naturally resilient multi-tasker with a super-heroic capacity for love and getting things done.*

**Defined by Us**

## Are You A Mum Ultrapreneur?

Well, if you're a Mum you already half way there, right? You probably already have all the skills and abilities you need to be a successful entrepreneur, or business mum, or WAHM (Work At Home Mum), or freelancer, or even a kitchen table tycoon. You choose the label. If you are in business for yourself and a mother, or are thinking about it, this book is for you. You are, or could be, a Mum Ultrapreneur.

Times and society are changing. Are you?

The whole underlying message from our book is (to quote Dr Phil) that if you keep on doing what you're doing, you'll keep on getting what you've got. This goes for absolutely anything in life...for individuals, corporations to Governments.

Both financially and morally maybe a change would be a good idea.

The traditional male view of business is about hierarchy, employers and employees, rules, procedures, loyalty and dedication. There are the bosses at the top and the workers below. Everyone knows their place, and more importantly their limitations. Everyone is paid according to their position and status. Some jobs are deemed through this to be less important than others and the occupiers of those less important roles have less of a voice. Remember it was only a few centuries ago that slavery was considered a viable workforce strategy!

Then western society started to realise that servitude brought mass abuses of power, wealth and influence. The people revolted – in some countries dramatically; think of the American War of Independence, French Revolution, the Russian Revolution, the Cultural Revolution. Society changed – became more egalitarian. Companies have changed too over the years; they had to.

Tom Peters and other gurus of the 1980s and 1990s spoke of shared goals, empowerment and managing diversity. Corporate and public personnel departments changed to human resources. Blue chip companies and local authorities alike brought in consultants to conduct branding exercises to unite employees and speak to their customers with a common voice. Top designers created new and expressive logos, and streets that crossed council boundaries had different coloured wheelie bins!

> *When a woman behaves like a man, why doesn't she behave like a nice man?*
> Edith Evans

Yet, at their heart these large companies remained emotionless layers of bosses and workers trapped in procedures and custom and practice. Goal setting was not empowering and motivating it became the be-all-and-end-all of the workplace. Those who thrived (albeit temporarily) were testosterone-pumped and target-happy.

Greed is good quoted Gordon Gecko famously in the film Wall Street. Executive burnout became a badge of honour. Times were changing and women could now enter the boardroom (if their shoulder pads allowed them to get through the door!) but at what cost?

> *At work, you think of the children you have left at home. At home, you think of the work you've left unfinished. Such a struggle is unleashed within yourself. Your heart is rent.*
> **Golda Meir**

Career or family? That was the choice. Long hours and total commitment are required on both sides so they didn't mix very well.

Shareholders and company executives understandably embraced diversity. After all. they didn't care who made them the millions – male or female, black or white, working class barrow boy or public school toff. Just give up your life and your identity, they said; make us rich and we will shower you in Porsche 911s and penthouse suites (oh, and as much cocaine as you can snort - you'll need it to keep the pace up!).

The bubble had to burst and of course it did – enter the recession of the early Nineties. But did we learn? Some of us did. Despite the economic slide during the respite of the late Nineties and the early Noughties new breeds of employer stepped forward.

Men and women abandoning the material-rich/time and creativity-poor world of large corporations to set up on their own. Now, of course there have always been entrepreneurs but today more and more of them are women and more importantly mothers. What is the secret to their success?

> *All mothers are working mothers.*
> **Unknown**

Well, it's a myth that mothers have never had any business acumen. Looking back through history it would be probably impossible to find an era where mothers did not work. Even in the Victorian era middle class woman was responsible for the household - its budget and servants. The upper classes were not all indolent rich; many worked and schemed for the betterment of their families in accordance with a long tradition of wheeling and dealing in court, society and commerce.

As for the working classes - women worked in the factories, they tilled the land, they taught, they acted as wet nurses, and they took in sewing. With husbands dead on foreign shores many took over the running of inns and shops and let out rooms to gentlefolk.

I could go on and on.

Many working mums had to be creative household managers to feed and clothe their hordes of children, often whilst bearing more. Their husbands went down the mines, fought for their country abroad or emptied their wages into the coffers of the local hostelry! (Sorry, this is not supposed to be male bashing).

This strength, this determination, this creativity, this sense of purpose, this natural resilience is what lies behind the success of any Mum Ultrapreneur.

A total belief that problems can be solved. That no goal is too far and too high. That they will muck in and do whatever is required. That they are prepared to use whatever talents they possess to make their dreams a reality. The workforce is their family. Their aim is to be of service. They offer high standards because that's what they expect from their own. Therefore they naturally motivate and encourage all to play their part. They find niche markets. They listen to their customers and meet their needs. Their fulfilment comes from the business/family being successful and growing stronger each day and the financial rewards are a bonus for, not the *raison d'etre* of, their commitment.

For businesses to survive in this new age, they will have to actively find the rough diamonds amongst us and cut them skilfully. By valuing the hidden SPARKLE as only a mother can; nurturing the talent of the individual to their true strengths and working with apparent weaknesses. And if your business isn't doing that consider carefully why you are still there or are planning to return. Most of us work to live but imagine waking up each morning excited by the day and actually living to work?

It's time to focus on the solution not the problem.

Can you think of a better way?

*Mama exhorted her children at every opportunity to 'jump at de sun.' We might not land on the sun, but at least we would get off the ground.*

Zora Neale Hurston

## Susan's View: The Birds & The Bees!

When Mark and I first discussed this book I was buzzing with ideas. Then I lost faith. Then Mark started writing Gemma's story. Then I started buzzing with lots of ideas again. Then once more become distracted. Then Mark sent the idea off to publishers and got some really positive feedback. Then I got scared. Then Mark and I discussed how we could add even more value to the book and guess what..? Buzzing again! Mark would get up before 5am to write. I would get up at 6.30am to beat the kids to the bathroom and my day as a working Mum would begin. Mark would send me drafts. I would read them, buzz a bit and then find something more important to do like cleaning out the fridge – well, eating the contents in order to one day clean out the fridge...possibly...one day...when I get time...

It was an interesting dynamic.

It felt very one-sided. Mark seemed to be doing all the work. I buzzed!

Like many of you I have ideas, lots of them, but most remain as a bee trapped in a glass. I can see the way ahead. I have a total desire to get there. I buzz and buzz but then give up.

Mark was the one who lifted my glass. Why? Because he believed in me and this project. Mark believes in the wisdom of women in a way far greater than most women believe in themselves. That's why I wanted to collaborate with him on this book and share this wisdom with others. Here are stories of inspiring women, who overcame external, and even harder still, internal obstacles.

Perhaps you are able to lift your own glass. If so, that's fantastic and you have my total admiration.

The rest of us need a helping hand.

Perhaps from a friend, a partner or a family member; it may be born out of necessity or forced upon us by outside events; it might be this book.

But I have learnt, through putting this book together and talking to over 30 Mum Ultrapreneurs, that once the glass is lifted, you're out - there is no turning back.

Again I cite the writing of this book as an example. Over the summer I arranged all the phone interviews and with each interview my confidence in this project grew. It became my passion and took over everything until the end result is what you are holding in your hand.

There's a wonderful side effect to this self-belief - as we grow to have faith in ourselves we increase our belief in others - and them in us. It is incredible.

Within the workplace we do not want to or need to become better than men in a male-dominated world.

We can realise our own value and the value of those around us and manage that effectively. We set our own standards, our own rules.

*Mum Ultrapreneur* is about women embracing their gifts and the skills and talents of others. It's not about excluding men nor wishing to emulate them. It is all about taking the rough diamond inside each of us and allowing it to sparkle.

Marianne Williamson is quoted as saying (also attributed to Nelson Mandela):

*Our deepest fear is not that we are inadequate.*

*Our deepest fear is that we are powerful beyond measure.*

*It is our light, not our darkness that most frightens us.*

*We ask ourselves, who am I to be brilliant, gorgeous, talented and fabulous?*

*Actually, who are you not to be?*

*You are a child of God.*

*Your playing small doesn't serve the world.*

*There is nothing enlightened about shrinking so that other people won't feel insecure around you.*

*You were born to make manifest the glory of God within us.*

*It's not just in some of us; it's in everyone.*

*And, as we let our own light shine,*

*We unconsciously give other people permission to do the same.*

*As we are liberated from our fear, Our presence automatically liberates others.*

Good eh?

But the everyday reality is that millions of women (and men) are *not* shining. Before sitting down to write this I spoke to an old friend. She is a great writer, a wonderful word-smith, with amazing ideas, and also a lovely person.

But during our conversation, instead of outlining all the reasons why she should send that fantastic story she sent me off to a publisher, she spent nearly half an hour outlining all the chores she had to do first. She spoke of not having the time to write because she needed to work to feed the family and then spend the rest of the time feeding them. So when could she write? And how could she be so selfish as to bury her head in her books when her children's clothes needed ironing! I suggested she view writing as a way to feed her children. And perhaps, should she earn enough, she could pay someone else to do the ironing?

*Mum Ultrapreneur* is about applying a different wisdom to our everyday reality. On a training course I was running, the other day, one woman asked me why all management books were written by men. The best answer I could give her was to say that I know books by female writers do exist but, sadly, they are not as common as those written by men and in many cases not so well-championed, so one may have to look beyond the shelves of W H Smith to find them. And, actually,... as it happens, I'm writing one... but, only because a man saw that I had wisdom to share.

Contrast the conversation I had with my writer friend above with one I had with a young male colleague. Though only a temp for my organisation during the summer holidays, when he returned to university he boasted to me that he had found a job running a bar.

'Wow, you're *running* the bar?' I gasped.

'Well, not exactly...' he replied with rediscovered modesty.

'You're collecting the empties then?'

'Hmm... yes but...'

I have been on many interview panels where the male interviewees have bigged up their contribution to projects and tasks whereas their more experienced female counterparts have played down theirs, speaking of we, us and the team. To quote Oprah Winfrey:

> *Being a mother is the hardest job on earth.*
> *Women everywhere must declare it so.*

I suspect many women do not realise or appreciate their contribution, their gifts and talents. Are you one of them?

Women are certainly less likely to believe that anyone else would be interested in hearing about their ideas and dreams, which is a shame because, as the women in this book prove, our ideas are often good ones. And, as a mother, your skill set is amazing!

A comment I hear all the time is that it had to be done and that's it. No fanfares, no ticker tape parades. We boast less than men but that does not mean we have less to boast about. Of course there are glorious exceptions to this we can all think of – go on, what names can you conjure up? Marie Curie, Margaret Thatcher, Anita Roddick, J.K.Rowling, Sharon Osbourne?

> *Women are the real architects of society.*
> Harriet Beecher Stowe

This book celebrates the wisdom that women, especially mothers, hold within themselves. This is both a personal wisdom and one which has passed on through generations.

We have raised families. We have created societies. We have supported our men and our children for generations. We are exceptional organisers, empowering managers and motivating educators. And now woman are proving themselves to be outstanding and inspirational entrepreneurs. 'Here come the girls' is not only a catchy Sugar Babes hit; it is actually happening in front of our very eyes today.

But, having said all that, I believe that it's not purely a gender thing. There is something about being a *parent* which makes a difference. It's not about being a woman, though we must not play down natural feminine business savvy, it's about being responsible and needing to find a way. A stay-at-home Dad is as likely to develop this instinctive knowledge. The important thing is to realise that you have what it takes to succeed inside you right now, this minute. And you need to believe that you can do it.

If you can survive the first year of your child's life, c'mon, you can do anything!

## Mark's View: There's Always A Way

So why would a man write passionately about the virtues of women in business? What's wrong with sticking to football, fast cars and porn with a little added gang violence? Personally I can think of a million and one reasons why a man must attempt at least to appreciate and be grateful for a woman's touch, metaphorically of course!

But first let's make one thing perfectly clear from the start; our intention is *not* to create a male-bashing book, proclaiming every woman is great and men are totally useless, except for the washing up! Neither are we calling for the total feminisation of the workplace - far from it.

I want to encourage mothers to go for it because the world of business needs you. It is not for everyone. Being an entrepreneur requires passion and drive and a lot of hard work but if anyone is naturally predisposed to making the dream a reality, it's a mother.

Becoming a father has totally transformed my life, and though I have worked hard in my businesses, I am permanently exhausted looking at my mother and wife and seeing how they make it all happen. No obstacle is too big – there is always a way.

Within my own little world I've had monetary success; though I had worked hard I must admit it was mainly because I was in the right place at the right time. My father and I had over 50 bricklayers across South East London and Kent working their proverbials off for over 12 years. I never really worried where the money would come from; I knew it would arrive week after week to pay the mounting wage bill and give me a very good lifestyle. Now that is the power of the Law of Attraction. I believed. I was grateful. I looked out for everyone I came in contact with. It was a good fun time.

But, and there's always a but! I wanted to expand the business, work with other contractors and create our own development company, thinking the best way forward was partnering with others. This could and should have been a good strategy. But, unwittingly, I gave my trust away and allowed myself to be compromised, unaware I was exposing my family and self to a gamble.

The new contractors and venture partners both turned out to be less than honourable (at about the same time too!). My generosity and kindness had been taken as a sign of weakness in a male dominated arena and I, along with my family paid the price in full.

The Bank pulled the plug on my overdraft and closed all our accounts including my six-month-old daughter's. The Tax man knocked on the door the day before Christmas Eve to take £20,000 of anything he could get.

My savings dwindling, I focused on survival, scraping change together from my girls' piggy banks and not answering the door to the window cleaner to save what cash and face I had left! The more I concentrated on surviving the more I survived. Another powerful lesson, hope you are taking notes? The Law of Attraction gives you back what you focus on 100% of the time.

It took a little persistence to turn things around (thank goodness for the internet) but it has happened. Though I will probably make the odd mistake here and there in the future, one thing I am certain of is that I will never make the same one again, and I hope I am a better person and father for enduring the tougher times.

We all have our own stories of our battles and we have no choice but to soldier on. But the key is the spirit with which we do it. Winston Churchill got it right when he said that success is moving from failure to failure with enthusiasm. We will eventually get to where we want to go in life, once we have decided where this is.

On consideration, throughout my own little trials and tribulations there has always been the guiding North Star of my family, especially my wife and mother. Though dark clouds obscured it, and I stubbornly refused to take cover from the storms, it remained bright and steadfast.

And that's where the wisdom behind this book resides.

I trusted so-called experts with letters after their names, and ignored the people who knew me best, and my own inner wisdom. I now know that there is a better way. The way of the *Mum Ultrapreneur*.

Beginning at home, I am truly amazed how much my wife, Sarah, achieves in such a short space of time. I have to get up two hours earlier in the morning to keep up (yes, I am writing this at some ungodly hour before everyone gets up!) But very soon she will overtake me as I head off to work; she'll be getting the kids up, washed, dressed and fed, then getting ready herself, whilst tidying the house, already knowing what we are having for dinner tonight, finding time to check her email or doing a little urgent ironing if she feels the need. Then after dropping the kids off to school she'll head off to her nearly full-time job, before starting the whole process back in reverse. Need I go on? (If I did she'll think I'm after something!) But I think she's inspiring and cherish my life with her.

*There was never a great man who had not a great mother – it is hardly an exaggeration.*
Olive Schreiner

Then there is my own mother who has become one of the most prolific salespeople in her chosen field, at the age of 59 she is still getting better and better. She often earns more in her three or four-day week than most people earn in a month; whilst still giving her own children and grandchildren her love and support. She's in no rush to retire - she enjoys her work. I must add she has never read a sales technique book or attended a sales seminar. Everything she does is natural, comes from the heart and she achieves a win-win scenario in a refreshingly honest way.

Finally, there are my beautiful daughters, Emma and Amelia, who fill my heart with a smile every single hour of the day (of course I'm not biased in any way!).

Being fortunate enough to have all of the above in my life started my inquisitive mind ticking over. Of course my family are unique and very special to me. But the actions of both my wife and mother are being duplicated millions of times over every day up and down the country – indeed, the world!

So why with all this natural ability flowing around us do we all continue to take it for granted or only appreciate it when it's too late? Also, as importantly, why do businesses fail to recognise it and consistently fail to harness or imitate these strengths? It beats me, but if I, an ex-bricklayer, can recognise and appreciate what's staring me in the face, then so why can't the average CEO?

> Susan's quick note: *'cos most of them are men, probably!*

Maybe it's time for them to step aside and make way for the new CEO on the block. She has always been there, waiting to pick up the pieces when things go wrong and supporting us at our most vulnerable times. She was also there when we were on our winning streaks, when we could do no wrong, sharing our visions and hopes... so maybe we should have listened a little harder when we were growing up...

As well as these women, there's now a new brand of Mum on the horizon. Much more confident, she doesn't need a power suit to conform to the old hierarchy or centuries of past conditioning... as a Mum Ultrapreneur, she can spot an opportunity a mile away.

Mum Ultrapreneurs are not necessarily high flyers heading million dollar companies.. From childminders and decorators to the Mums who do a little selling on eBay or those who dabble in multi-level networking companies for a few hours a week, they are all out there, running a home and family at the same time, of course. This emerging economy is primarily serviced based, nurtures relationships and has no formal hierarchical culture; it's safe to say the Jimmy Choos are well and truly on the other foot now.

We are not alone in recognising the value of feminine and maternal attributes in the workplace. Take the little quiz below and see if you need more proof?

Who manages many things at once?

- Who puts effort into their appearance?
- Who usually takes care of the detail?
- Who asks the most questions in a conversation?
- Who is a better listener?
- Who is interested in communication skills?
- Who is inclined to get involved?
- Who encourages harmony and agreement?
- Who has intuition?
- Who works with a long to-do list?
- Who enjoys a recap of the day's events?
- Who's better at keeping in touch with others?

Do we really need to tell you the answer? Of course not.

That quick quiz appears on the back cover of the book *Selling Is a Woman's Game: Fifteen Powerful Reasons Why Women Can Outsell Men*, by Nicki Joy and Susan Kane-Benson, coming to our attention via Tom Peters' fantastic book on *Leadership*.

Hits the nail firmly on the head, wouldn't you agree?

If women have always worked, had own their own businesses or carved out pioneering careers and achieved great things, and if women are ultra - capable beings, why are there so few Mum Ultrapreneurs?

Being an entrepreneur is not for everyone but don't dismiss the idea straight away, bear with us awhile longer. Maybe that spirit is not within you but what can you do to get a better deal if you go back to work? Do you know your rights? Can you be as committed and effective now you have other priorities?

Can you really have it all? We would like to believe you can.

Whatever your decision do you believe you can set the world on fire?

Great!

Let's carry on then...

## Man, woman, cat, dog... we all SPARKLE

> *No one can make you feel inferior without your consent.*
> Eleanor Roosevelt

Remember no one is asking anyone to dig out the red cape and start putting your Bridget Jones pants outside your Lycra tights (unless it helps of course). Relax and listen to your inner voice.

Think back to when you were a child. Conditioning starts very young. There are pink and blue romper suits for starters, and then girls' and boys' toys. Some of us may even have buried deep within us painful memories of not being allowed to play with either Action Man or Barbie because it was not gender appropriate. But this is not about having a natural predilection for cerise or khaki, it's about learning at a very, very young age to conform. To follow the rules. To suppress your true self to fit in or receive love or avoid punishment.

*Mum Ultrapreneur* is not a psychology book where we ask you to dig deep and work out all your past traumas. This section is simply a request to be open to the idea that the person walking around today may not be the real you!

The real you knows when you are false and will keep trying to subvert all your efforts to go against your true nature. The real you, for want of a better analogy, can be called your soul. This is where your SPARKLE resides.

We all have this SPARKLE. Men, women, cats, dogs, sunflowers...everything on this planet has its own unique SPARKLE.

Every pebble, each and every grain of sand of the beach is unique.

This SPARKLE is the brilliant difference that sets everything apart. Even man-made items have odd flaws or marks that give them their own personality.

## Susan's Note

As a child I knew my Mum loved me BUT always suspected she loved my younger brother more. As a child I believed that she must have a favourite like I had a favourite doll or teddy.

When I had my first child I remember being overwhelmed with the unconditional love I felt for him. It was the most powerful thing I had ever experienced and I am sure most parents feel the same. It's impossible to describe this love to anyone who has not had a child. Like the relentless sleepless nights, no one can prepare you for the impact it will have on your life.

When pregnant with Number Two I was worried about how I would be able to give the same level of love to her. I lived in a world of limits and boundaries where everything is rationed because there is not enough to go around. (This was before I discovered the truth that in fact we live in a universe falling over itself to give us all that we desire.) I was anxious right up to the delivery.

But there I was holding my beautiful daughter, admittedly drugged up to the eyeballs (me, not the baby), sobbing all over again with the same rush!

And again with babies three and four. Each of them, as they have grown, despite their shared DNA, is an individual. The only thing they share is their surname. Sometimes I like one more than another because, as different personalities, we clash or agree on various points, but the love remains solid and unchanging.

What does all this have to do with finding one's SPARKLE?

Well, *Mum Ultrapreneur* is about embracing our wisdom as mothers – right? That wisdom has been passed down through the ages but equally has been conditioned. Parents, because they love us, will have wanted the best for us. Given the perceived societal wisdom of the time and their upbringing etc. they may have not always given the best advice or guided us along the right path. Equally because we are different and SPARKLE in our own ways they may not have understood how certain advice and actions rather than polishing the SPARKLE within us actually poured rivers of mud over its brilliance.

> *Every finger is not the same length,*
> *nor every son the same deposition.*
> **Traditional Irish Saying**

*Mum Ultrapreneur* is about reminding ourselves of the good stuff. The nurturing, warm, supportive role our mothers should have played in our lives and, whether or not this was our reality as children, as adults we can embrace this innate knowledge and use it in our family and business dealings to create a supportive, fully functioning, sparkling life.

Eleanor Roosevelt was right. Please don't let anyone rob you of your shine, it's in each and every one of us.

We all have the right to SPARKLE.

# Growing Family, Growing Business, Growing Stronger

OK, now for the statistics. Google 'Business Mums', 'Women Entrepreneurs', 'Kitchen Table Tycoon' (as coined by the London School of Economics) or 'Mumpreneur 'and you will find a comprehensive list of potentially helpful websites with advice, success stories and useful links.

BT Yell.com even has its own site dedicated to entrepreneurial mums. In 2008 they commissioned a survey of over 200 business mums and a free report is available to download from their site. Here are some of their stats:

- Mums who run their own business contribute £4.4bn to the UK economy.
- 13% felt ready for new challenges.
- 26% felt that negotiation skills were improved through the process of caring for children and managing their needs and wants.
- 36% believed that bringing up children sharpened their ability to focus on one particular task right through to completion.
- 40% said the drive and desire to run their own business came while they were pregnant or within a year of their baby being born.
- 40% said pregnancy changes their priorities and they wanted to be based at home.
- 43% believed they were more able to deal with difficult situations since becoming a mother.

- 53.9% found that having children made them better at thinking ahead and planning.
- 75% reckoned they had developed improved multi-tasking skills since having a child.
- 92% believed having and looking after their children improved their work skills.
- It is a very interesting report and well worth a read. It also states that 36% were aged between 26 and 30; 48% opt to go it alone while a further 37% set up with their partners.
- But the most important statistic is that, whilst 74% of the women surveyed had left traditional employment, a whopping 73% felt satisfied or very satisfied with their decision and 66% are more satisfied running their own business than in their previous job.

The range of businesses was vast, with child-minding being the most common home-based start up for mums. Money is not a major incentive for most mums. Although it is encouraging to note that in 2007 Barclays Wealth Management predicted that women millionaires would out number their male counterparts by 2010. They cited kitchen table companies as a major contributor to this.

So, if you decide to set up on your own you will be in excellent company. In Part Three we have excerpts from interviews with amazing Mum Ultrapreneurs and a true-life case study of one, Karen, who had a good, pensionable job and gave it up to set up as a child-minder. She is now working as a event manager and website designer with her own company.

Whatever the service or product, whatever your good idea, you can do it if you want to.

Gone are the days when mums stayed at home because it was taboo to go back to work. Employers are becoming more family friendly. But there is a third way... set up from your home.

How you use the rest of this book is totally up to you.

You can read it systematically from cover to cover.

You can skip straight to Part Three and dip in and out of the wonderful Mum Ultrapreneur interview quotes (and then visit *www.mum-ultrapreneur.com/bonuses* to listen to the interviews in full).

You can snuggle up with cup of tea and a bar of chocolate and read Gemma's fictional story in Part Two.

Or, if you already bursting with ideas and want to get going, jump to Part Four, where you will find a range of questions to inspire and test your ideas and a list of further reading.

Or mix it up and keep coming back to the bit that works for you.

Whatever you choose to do we hope you enjoy reading about amazing Mums like you, who want a better life for themselves and their children. And we hope that you realise you have options. You can be whatever you want to be.

It is possible to have a family and business life that SPARKLES!

Before moving on consider the following:

> *It is not until you become a mother, that your judgement slowly turns to compassion and understanding.*
> Erma Bombeck

You will find our personal recipe on how to SPARKLE on the following pages, and though you will find some of the methods are common sense, please keep in mind that doesn't mean it is common practice.

By applying these ingredients in a way that suits you and becoming aware of your own uniqueness and purpose you will forever shine.

Just as important though, you may well become more conscious of the abundance of hidden talent all around you and encourage other people to sparkle even more.

Remember, the greatest leaders are not bothered about others stealing their thunder. Far from it; their whole being is concentrated on bringing the talents of others to the surface.

Very similar to parenthood wouldn't you agree? So enjoy the rest of the book and share what you learn here with others just like you.

*You don't really understand human nature unless you know why a child on a merry-go-round will wave at his parents every time around – and why his parents will always wave back.*

**William D. Tammeus**

Susan Ödev & Mark Weeks

# Part Two

# Gemma's Story

## 1: Keep it Simple ~~Stupid~~ ... Sexy!

## Life $\underline{S}$PARKLES

*Questioning is the door of knowledge.*
Traditional Irish saying

*Remember always to trust your own heart.*
*Everything will be fine. SPARKLE!*

Originally Gemma had thought these words, written by her Nan on her 18th birthday card, were the ramblings of a dear old lady wanting to ease the inner turmoil of a spotty teenager. But now, some 18 years later, sitting on her bed flicking through old family albums, birthday cards and other little keepsakes Gemma had the strangest feeling. Her pulse quickened and her skin tingled with goose bumps of excitement. She reread the text and felt inspired; for the first time in years.

'Of course, why didn't I think of that before,' she cried, remembering the proud old lady sitting in her favourite armchair by the window; on the sill were the usual pack of Embassy Players, Murray mints and brandy & coke. Maybe Nan was a little pickled but at 86 she still had a twinkle in her eye and a mind sharper than most. Gemma laughed a little to herself ... then felt a sharp twinge in her belly.

'Okay, okay I know you're here, how can I forget? You've been cooking in there nicely for six months!' Smiling to herself she gently stroked her belly and thought, 'Number three, and it doesn't get any easier.'

'But hopefully it will be better...' Gemma knew these moods were mainly hormonal but it had to be different this time. After all, this time she knew what she was doing...right? And she was finally with the right man...right? Third time lucky...right?

The past few years had been a roller coaster. 'Life is, I suppose...' Gemma mused. 'But it wasn't as much fun as Ronan Keating would have us believe!'

Gemma had felt helpless as she watched the collapse and closure of her independent estate agency. Everything happened at once, or so it seemed. The death of her father, her husband's affair, the credit crunch, the dreaded Home Information Packs, fewer and fewer sales, increased rates, higher utility and advertising costs... the list seemed endless. In the space of a year Gemma's world had caved in and her dream business had disappeared.

She developed an aura of pessimism and gloom. Even her closest friends were starting to exclude her from their usual gatherings as they found the only thing she ever talked about was her rotten luck. This only helped reaffirm her belief that the world was against her.

But who could blame her? For Gemma, breaking free from her old firm and starting her own business had taken every drop of her courage. And the triumph she felt initially was short lived. The whole process was unbelievably stressful. Her ex-husband, Rob, had been unsupportive; telling her time and time again she was stupid to try and go it alone. Was he right?

Tears welled in Gemma's eyes as she recalled, with inappropriate intensity for such a distant memory, Rob's response when she asked him to pick up the kids from the child-minder's, just once.

'Childcare is your problem!'

'But I'm stuck across town, the clients arrived late but they were really interested. I think they're going to buy. They asked lots of questions. Now the rush hour traffic has kicked in. The child-minder charges when I'm late and it's on your way.'

'I told you that if you wanted to do this – your first priorities are the kids and me. You agreed. If you can't handle it...'

'Yes, but...'

Gemma shook herself and thought, 'I don't need to think about all that now. That is not my reality. I am a good mother. I am an able woman. I was a great estate agent! The problem was just the timing, and it should have worked. Would have worked. *Will* work!'

Undeterred she had continued, despite the worsening economy, vowing never to return to her old estate agency job or anything else, for that matter, which was built upon the Old Boy network.

To fit in at Brown, Gordon and Ramsey she had to act like one of the lads – which even the lads found difficult to do. High achievers at BG&R worked ridiculously long hours. Over-inflated commission rates, successfully won, were badges of honour. It was seen as a sign of weakness when Gemma skipped the liquid lunches, preferring to grab a bite to eat before her next appointment. But those lunches were often where the deals were done. And failure to attend weekly debriefing sessions in the Dog and Ferret was a grave source of concern for Messrs Gordon and Ramsey, though Mr. Brown said that he understood that such places were not suitable for a young lady after dark.

At the time Gemma had felt compelled not to shake the olive tree, as her Italian grandmother would say. And with Rob between jobs she was hoping for promotion. If successful she could then make changes in her own department.

But it wasn't meant to be.

Simon, the biggest toad of all, and, worse, five years her junior, pipped her to the post. This was the last straw. It was a case of jump, now or never. Gemma had even started to sense, to her disgust, that her language and mannerisms were starting to resemble those of the lads! It took a monumental leap of faith but... she jumped.

The only person to believe in her at the time was her father, but now even he had gone. He had filled her head with stories of entrepreneurs who had succeeded on their own terms and had changed the world into a better place. The one story that captivated her was that of Dame Anita Roddick, whose well worn book *Business as Unusual* lay by her bedside as a constant reminder that dreams do come true. Much to her Mum's disapproval she had grown up with her Dad drilling into her the belief that 'Imagination is more important than knowledge'.

And that if she could believe in something she could achieve it. Well she had believed in it, tried harder than ever before, but still things didn't go to plan.

Breathing a heavy sigh she placed all her keepsakes back into her battered tin and whispered to herself: ' maybe,' as she took one final glimpse at her Nan's words of encouragement and hope.

Later that evening Gemma was wondering when it was that the Coven last managed to get together?

The Coven was formed on October 31 1991 when six unlikely friends shared a house at university. It had met regularly since; the gatherings ensuring hours of amusement, chat and mutual support.

How miserable she had been that last time, no wonder no one has attempted to arrange another meeting.

But so much has changed since then, Gemma thought. I hadn't even met Ryan and I'm now six months gone with his child! ... Everyone has been so busy... it must be two years, at least... well; it's time to change that. Let them see Gems is back!

Gemma felt she had a lot to be thankful for. Her two children, Sam and Katie were happy, healthy and even if she did say so herself, very beautiful. There was the unquenchable love of her mother and sister Jayne to be truly thankful for. Though not as close as they had been, they were always there for each other. And now she had Ryan.

Ryan was Gemma's first real love. If she were honest - her only love. Fate had brought them back together again. Who would have predicted taking a short-term contract as an administrative assistant for the local council would bring Ryan back into her life?

A broken lift led to her calling in the engineers, a job delegated to her at random; the maintenance contract was with Ryan's firm.

He was part of the second wave, called in to solve the problems the first battalion of engineers had failed to sort out. Gemma was taking minutes in the office next door and almost missed him completely when he arrived.

As she walked back to her desk, the lift doors opened and standing before her, in a halo of fluorescent down-lighting, Ryan stood – a vision in blue dungarees.

And now she was having his baby.

It was not where she expected to be after all that had happened. Of all the painful losses of the last few years nothing compared to the bitter divorce from Rob. Gemma had eventually won custody of the kids and things were settling down. Only now could she see how toxic her marriage had been.

Yes, she had a lot to be thankful for and it was time to get the Coven back together to celebrate. Gemma fished out her mobile from her handbag and dialled excitedly.

Tulip? Yes, it's me Gems... fancy a girls' night out? ... Yes, the whole Coven... Fantastic! I'll call the others and text you my new address. Love you.'

> *No man ever wore a scarf as warm as his daughter's arm around his neck.*
> Old Irish saying

As she laid some A4 pads out across the kitchen table, several pictures fell to the floor face up. There was one of a beautiful looking villa in the South of France, high up in the hills, with breathtaking views out to the Mediterranean; the other a snapshot of her sitting on her father's broad shoulders, aged about seven, during a Spanish family holiday.

Gemma gazed at that familiar smile and wished he was here now.

The pictures remained on the floor as Gemma was finding it difficult to bend today. She'll wait for Ryan to come in from the garden. He was still having fun with Sam and Katie - she could hear the laughter from the kitchen and it reminded her of her childhood.

What a contrast to the sounds of only a few years ago. There was plenty of laughter during the day after school but there was an unnatural silence when Rob came home.

Gemma understood he was tired but she had been working too!

Sometimes she really resented Rob crashing in front of the TV the moment he came home. Most nights he hadn't even the energy to take a shower so the room would reek of sweat and Castrol GTX. The weekends were no better with seemingly endless tirades about muddy boots, scattered toys and boisterous games. Gemma recalled the opening words of a book she had once read: *To the worm living in horseradish, the world is horseradish.*

Only a few years ago that had been her reality.

'That's how life was,' she thought 'I never considered it could be different. …. yet my childhood was so very different – how did I let that go on so long?

Her thoughts returned to her pads. Though several weeks had passed since she had reread her Nan's words they hadn't entirely left her:

## *Remember always to trust your own heart. Everything will be fine. SPARKLE!*

Gemma had made several notes to herself in the meantime but had never made the time to sit down and really think ahead. But today she felt upbeat and truly energised. Gemma promised that this would be the first day of the rest of her life (which it was…)

She had made goals and plans before, which had helped her focus a little, although they had never inspired her and always seemed impractical. Why was that?

Gemma had always loved reading fiction and for a brief period even enjoyed non-fiction self-development books.

Her father had books everywhere: the toilet, garage, cupboard under the stairs, his car. He even kept an old copy of Think and Grow Rich in his bedside drawer.

Gemma could still hear her Mum joking, 'All these bloody Get Rich books lying around, maybe if I sold them we *would* be rich!'

Her father would flash his usual smile and be on to his next idea.

All these memories were a lifetime ago, when times seemed so simple. No, I'm not getting to that age, am I? she thought and started shaking her head, of course not. Gemma smiled, and then allowed herself to drift back off in her thoughts.

Everything in her childhood had a certain amount of order. Her mother and father complimented each other perfectly and their home had always been a place filled with love and laughter. The family spent so much time together. A tear formed; she felt a bit woozy. It was as if undulating blobs of sadness and happiness were colliding against each other.

Hormones!

Then, thinking aloud: Beautiful memories of the past may be wonderful, but I can't get stuck in it. Take the lesson and move on. Down the left hand column of a piece of paper, in bold letters she wrote her Nan's favourite word:

S
P
A
R
K
L
E

She pictured her mother buzzing around always doing something and keeping up everyone's spirits. Why had Mum always been her happiest after a good clean out? She would love to turn the house upside down and get rid of any clutter. Also every year she would surprise Dad by booking a skip and announcing 'Guess what we're doing this weekend!'

Yet Dad seemed to have a sixth sense about these rampages and always sneaked his magazines and books to their usual hiding places in time!

Or Mum and Jayne would have mad tidying sprees singing *A Spoonful Of Sugar* in faux Julie Andrews style, in ever higher and shriller voices, clicking their fingers as they worked. If it didn't move it got dusted, boxed or binned.

Gemma never had the same gusto as her mother or Jayne for having a clear out. She struggled with the notion of throwing things away and keeping things tidy.

'What made me think of that?'

Gemma returned to the letters she had written…

S
P
A
R
K
L
E

The kids' laughter in the garden evaporated as she searched her mind for clues. Her Nan had always come out with strange old sayings, many of which seemed wise, yet after the umpteenth brandy she would also recall sharing nine to a bed and scooping mugs of tea out of metal buckets! It gave her Nan great pleasure to remember the times when everyone pulled together, made enormous sacrifices, but never gave up.

'Of course,' she exclaimed, 'Everything was simple then.'

She grabbed her pen and next to the S she jotted down...

S = Simple

She thought for a second then put a line through it and scrawled...

S = ~~Simple~~ Simplicity

'Now that's better.'

On reflection, both her grandmothers had a truckload of sayings. Her Nonni's spirit lived on in Gemma's mother who often mixed up Italian and English expressions. Her Irish Nan, she suspected, made most of her proverbs up. When she and Jayne were fighting she would say 'There's a pair of you there as the Devil said to his horns!'

Eh? What on earth did that mean?

SPARKLE could be an acronym, wow like SMART!

What will the other letters stand for? Simplicity made sense. If Gemma could make her life a little simpler, and appreciate what she had now, she would be able to refocus herself and totally allow herself to be what she wanted to be!

She grabbed her pen and made brief, random, notes. She produced a stream of seemingly unconnected words and phrases and found it very inspiring...

## SIMPLICITY

- Must try to de-clutter my life.
- Be grateful for everything in my life.
- Minimalist attitude – how much stuff do I really need, including money?
- 80/20 principle – Pareto's? I must reread Dad's book again!
- Prioritise!!!

- Clutter – Recycle, reuse, re-clutter?
- Simple – Simple ideas, simple words, keep it simple.
- Don't bombard myself with trivia and trash, including TV.
- Sort out my bank statements.
- File all important documents properly – manage my money better.
- Sort out my wardrobe – better keep all my shoes though!
- If I struggle or can't face throwing things away - GET MUM ROUND!

Gemma was on a roll but no sooner had she turned to a clean page than Ryan bounded through the open French doors with Katie and Sam, one under each arm giggling their heads off.

'Look what I've caught for lunch!'

She closed her book and joined in.

'Great, I'm starving!'

## 2: Eureka!

# Life SP_ARKLE_S

*A journey of a thousand miles
starts with a single step.*[2]
**The Buddha**

Gemma scanned the pages of Ryan's Sunday rag:

**"Oil Surges To Biggest Single Day Advance"**
**"Britain's Rail Network To Be Cut by 14%"**
**"$CO^2$ Cost Warning"**

...and in the left hand column...

**15,000 estate agency jobs will be lost this
year as the housing market crisis takes its toll.**

Breathing a heavy sigh she folded the paper and pushed it to the other side of the large oak table. She could empathise completely with all those who were going under, as she had, and wished she could help in some little way.

She remembered vividly the doom and gloom of the recession of the 1990s. Many people then questioned her career choice as an estate agent but it was the right move. She loved the job, was good at it and as the recession lifted so did her career prospects.

It always reared its ugly head within the construction and property sector months and months before hitting the average man and woman in the street. Why had no one learned from the past? she thought. Maybe it will always be this way while there remains a macho enthusiasm for boom and bust cycles, where the greed of a few leaves us all to suffer.

---

[2] Or a single email – that's progress!

This time things seemed different. Gemma sensed everyone and their dog had credit of some sort and it didn't take Einstein to recognise that the ripple effect in the sub-prime mortgage pools would turn into a remorseless tsunami.

Well, that's thinking positively! Gemma slapped herself gently on the hand. There, that's to remind me that what I think about I bring about. Wasn't Peter Jones the other night telling us all to stop talking ourselves into a recession? Perhaps with less telly I should stop reading the scaremongering papers as well!

It had been nearly a month since Gemma had decided that as well as trying to simplify her life, she would set herself some quiet time in the mornings before the house came alive. She had even dug out some of her dad's old books for a little inspiration. Some of these were now scattered around the table. She felt pleased with herself, already de-cluttered and now up with the lark, though a little tired. Gemma recalled her Mum tucking her up in bed:

> *Early to bed early to rise makes a poor man healthy, wealthy and wise!*

Being a mum was exhausting but it was also the greatest adventure in the world... probably. Gemma cherished every minute she had with her children, but her professional life still felt incomplete and the voices in her head were becoming ever louder.

So that's it. You failed and gave up. Is that the way you want the kids to remember you? The word *failure* kept coming back to haunt her.

In between spoonfuls of cereal Gemma would grab her pen and start writing the odd word to describe her mood. Though words were not flowing so well today she kept trying.

She turned her attention from her little note book to her A4 Black n' Red pad, which she now used as both her diary and new life planner. She called it her *Golden Notebook*.

On the very first page she had written her SPARKLE acronym. By the letter S she wrote Simplicity. Then on a clean page she jotted down the date at the top left and added:

> Today I'm Feeling:

Then leaving several lines wrote...

> I'm feeling anxious, frustrated, tired but happier, feel as though I should have achieved more with my life by now.

She paused for a second then scrawled,

> Notes for the day:

Under 'Notes for the day:' she paused.

Why do I feel so anxious?

The pregnancy?

The frightening mortgage repayments?

Or meeting the short term loan repayments that were taken out to stave off the inevitable end to her business?

All I do know is I am not a failure.

Then in large capital letters she wrote...

> I AM NOT A FAILURE,
> FAILING TO TRY IS FAILING!

Gemma recalled one of her dad's books on the Law of Attraction and had a quick look at the pile of books on the table for a little more encouragement.

> The more we focus our lives on the things we don't want the more of what we don't want turns up in our lives...by the truck load!

She added:

So get rid of negative thoughts, never complain and dwell on bad luck, stick such thoughts in your very own recycling bin - and focus on something you do want in your life.

No, don't recycle – DELETE!

I AM NOT A FAILURE,

I AM A SUCCESS!

If I achieved a certain level of success before I could do it again. But why should I put myself through it all again? Can't I be satisfied with a normal life?

Gemma gazed out of the kitchen window into the dark autumn morning. It was nearly 5.45 am and a few bedroom and bathroom lights started appearing from the street behind.

Was the daily grind of commuting for hours to get to work, shuffle paper around in a tedious job, then do it all again day after day really the way to live?

She knew the answer before her pen hit the paper.

> Living to work is not the way I am going to spend my life.

She wrote enthusiastically,

> I will fulfil my promises to myself... eventually.

Suddenly she stopped writing and shook her head slowly. Something wasn't right. She gazed at the pile of books in front of her and found herself reaching out for *The Street Kid's Guide To Having It All*.

She had read it very briefly and remembered something about The Natural Laws of the Universe. After a couple of minutes she put a line through the last few written words realising that even though her thoughts had been positive they were still sounding too far in the future. According to John Assaraf, for her life to truly change her thoughts and actions had to be spoken of in the present tense to be recognisable to the outside world and universe. Gemma quickly rewrote her thoughts.

I am now living life to the full and doing the work I love.

Followed by...

I am fulfilling my promises to myself.

She continued on the opposite page...

What am I great at that others find difficult?

Then leaving several lines...

If I had one dream business that could help improve the lives of others what would it be?

Finally she added,

What do people really want and how could I deliver it?

Drifting off in her thoughts she didn't hear Ryan creep up behind and gently kiss her neck. A delicious tingling sensation slithered down her body. She turned and saw his gleaming smile, ' Very funny,' she managed to blurt out, 'do you want me to have the baby right now?'

'No love, put the kettle on first,'

Ryan wrapped his arms around Gemma's shoulders giving her a gentle hug and whispered 'Love you.' Resting his chin on her shoulder Ryan started to read the few lines Gemma had wrote. She loved the warmth of his body and, as she was struggling with her thoughts this morning, his input would be much appreciated.

'Oh um, so this time you are out to change the world?'

'If you're going to bother to think you might as well think big,' she replied.

'I guess, but if you're busy changing the world... I had better put the kettle on.' Ryan released his hug. 'Toast?'

'I shouldn't, I had some cornflakes – see?' Gemma pushed the bowl across the table.

'C'mon, there's nothing in the world to compare with the taste of warm buttered toast, and the smell... mmm. Go on. I won't tell,' Ryan coaxed.

'Wait till you smell our newborn baby.' Gemma sat back smiling to herself as she patted her ever increasing bump. Ryan placed his hands on her belly gently.

'Can't wait – but I need something to eat now.' He laughed.

Before sitting down at the table Ryan took a scrap of paper and a pen from the kids' tin.

'Okay gorgeous, what's going through that brain of yours?'

Gemma loved his approach to life. Nothing was ever a big deal and he would always listen objectively to her thoughts without belittling her or putting her down. That, coupled with his confidence, was what she loved the most about him – oh and it helped that he was a pleasurable sight to behold even this early in the morning...

'I have to do something. It's obvious we both have to work. But the thing is I couldn't stand going through the motions of a job to exist. Also I don't want to wait for another seven months to get my act together. I want to get going today! I know the baby and the kids will take up most of my day but I feel I could do something different... you know I couldn't stand to return to the council – if I have to file another piece of paper I'll go mad!'

There was silence. Ryan had a slurp of tea.

She placed the A4 book in the middle of them both and then underlined the first question freehand.

What am I great at?

'Easy, do you want me to go first?' Ryan teased.

'Oi, be serious!'

'I am. Honest. Okay, let's think...You are creative, excellent with people and the kindest person I know. You are persistent to the point of being a royal pain in the backside. You are loyal and when you're on a roll your enthusiasm is contagious and your self-belief inspiring. So, if we can bottle all that... we can rule the world,'

Ryan did an embarrassing Mike Myers impersonation with his little finger hooked inside his mouth.

'I guess I am quite good at selling my ideas to others and I did love my little team fighting the giant corporate estate agents. We were on a mission. It was fun but hard work... and I really do miss it.'

'I know you do, babe, but times are changing,' Ryan pointed to the paper showing the intended job loses within the property sector.

'I guess so; I bet many will be independent agents too?'

'Yeah, I'm sure you're right. So what would your dream business be? Remember it is guaranteed to succeed and will be backed by Sir Richard Branson and Donald Trump. Failure is not an option.'

'Well, first I would gain the majority stake holding! I'm sure I could work my charm on both Sir Dick and the Don.'

They both laughed.

'I could focus on something along the lines of environmental issues or maybe the health and fitness industry? Whatever it turns out to be I think it will have to have a great web presence, allowing me to work wherever I happen to be and whenever I wanted to. So I guess it will be more service-orientated.'

'Sounds good, but then what?' Ryan prompted.

'This is the problem. I'm not sure what I do want or if I have the confidence to go for it all over again when I finally find out.'

Ryan reached out his hand to meet Gemma's and gave it a light squeeze, 'You've done it once before. You can do it again. This time you won't be alone. Whatever happens I will always stand by you.'

'Thanks,' she said holding back the tears for a change. 'The one thing I keep coming back to is property. With Dad in construction for so many years and Mum working in an estate agents it's in my blood.' She looked at Ryan.

'I think I know where this is going,' he responded, 'after family, property and people are your passion. But ... sometimes, you do go overboard ... on certain issues...'

'Okay, maybe that's the Irish/Italian in me. It's makes me very passionate and a little head strong, but I thought you liked that? Works a treat with Dick and Don.' Gemma chuckled as she grabbed her notebook and scribbled:

Passion! People! Property!

They both laughed and then together they heard a thud on the floor above and the sound of little footsteps scurrying their way downstairs. Before they knew it Sam was running into his mum's arms beaming a sunshine smile.

It was time to get on with the day.

*Le ore del mattino hanno l'oro in bocca.*
*Morning is the most precious time of day.*
**Italian saying**

Gemma dragged herself out of bed at the usual 5am and left Ryan snoring. With only nine weeks left before the baby arrived she wasn't sure how long she could maintain her routine. But with only a few weeks left at work, she was determined to last the course. She made notes during the day, in between endless meetings and relentless filing. Mentally she had already left her council job and with every tedious shuffle of paper she was more determined than ever not to return after maternity leave.

Despite the early start this was her sanctuary, when she could focus on what she wanted out of life. She was also getting into meditating. She had learned to love the majestic feeling of allowing her brain to drift on automatic pilot, revelling in the stillness. Yoga might be next on the list of things to try - seems to work for Madonna!

Again she sat alone at the kitchen table, making herself comfortable by placing a cushion behind the arch of her back, and then set the alarm clock on her phone to alert her after 20 minutes.

Taking a deep relaxing breath Gemma allowed herself to melt into the chair. She repeated in her mind 'breathing in love and light' on the in breath and 'breathing out negativity and all toxins' on the out breath.

Once fully relaxed Gemma imagined a white light flowing in through her feet from the earth below, its energy filling each cell as it moved through her legs and her thighs, then her back and stomach, up through her chest, shoulders and neck until finally moving gently up and out towards the heavens.

Filled with a renewed positive spirit she would picture her favourite place. Here her children laughed and played with Ryan in the dappled sunshine. The trees were heavy with blossom and the sound of a babbling brook provided the perfect sound track. Lying beside her was a healthy, giggling baby wrapped in a white shawl looking up with trusting eyes. She knew that all was right with the world and that here there were no fears, no doubts, and no hatred – only love and hope and joy.

Gemma repeated in her mind 'I love. I am loved. I am love.'

The alarm sounded with the stereophonic tones of Enrique Iglesias and Gemma inhaled one last time before reaching out and turning it off. It never ceased to amaze her how quickly the time went when she meditated and how great it made her feel for the rest of the day.

She had recently sent a series of emails on meditation to the Coven extolling how taking 20 minutes in the morning to focus on breathing could benefit so many areas of their lives. Most agreed it had certainly perked her up but they didn't have the time or inclination to try it for themselves. They would rather stay in bed another hour. Gemma remembered her Nan: 'You can lead a horse to water but you can't make it drink!'

Opening her A4 pad and reflecting on the notes she had made with Ryan yesterday quickened her pulse and Gemma could feel a flood of ideas pouring forward.

As she jotted down her simple page format Gemma was thinking of what Ryan had said. Yes she was passionate about her family, but, after that, her love of property and helping other people always seemed to dominate her life.

But what do others want? And how could she improve their lives once she had found the answer?

She rewrote her second question from Monday morning...

> If I had one dream business that could help improve the lives of others what would it be?

She started scribbling. Today she could feel the flow and wanted to get her ideas down on paper before they disappeared. Even if certain things didn't make sense at the time she knew it was all related in some magical way. She wrote for five minutes without taking her pen from the paper...

> Property is still the answer, but how can I help?
>
> How do I:
>
> - Connect to the 15,000 estate agents who are about to lose their livelihoods?
> - Give them hope?
> - Give the public value for money and a fantastic service?

The housing market is in the doldrums, mortgages are getting harder to come by, wages are stagnating, fuel and food costs continue to spiral upwards and first time buyers are practically non-existent. It's not very inspiring!'

> What's the answer?
>
> - Help people sell their homes faster and cheaper than others.
> - The internet....but a lot different from what is out there now.
> - Adding more options.
> - Sharing the pie with the workforce.
> - Build a family orientated environment.
> - Reward equals effort.

'That's it!'

Gemma could feel the excitement running through her. She was convinced even the baby got it! No hierarchy – partnership. Clients and agents are a team. The aim is to sell the house. Full stop. Introduce different concepts, even partner with auction houses, and be creative...

I think independent estate agents are the key.

She then left half a page and turned her attention to the last questions.

What does everyone want and how could I deliver it?

She jotted down...

> Everyone wants to be richer, but few are prepared to make a real effort. So if money doesn't do it... what does?

But few people ever feel they achieve any of these things.

Why is this?

Though her thoughts were very general a vivid picture was forming in her mind of how she could achieve something special.

> Deliver it by?

- Networking with existing agents, - build a new workforce.
- Flexible working hours.
- Internet orientated - give customers choice.
- Being HOT – Honest, Open, Trustworthy.
- Networking with potential clients/networking clubs.
- Making work a happier, more rewarding activity - something that makes getting out of bed in the morning a little easier.

Gemma stopped writing, reviewed her notes and thought to herself. Where did that all come from? I haven't even had a cup of tea yet!

Her head was spinning. She wanted to go and wake Ryan up but she hesitated. First she would add a little more structure to her thoughts. She still had nearly an hour.

Gemma returned back to the table and made herself comfortable, her thoughts racing again as soon as she touched her pen.

She wrote the words:

I follow my passion and heart.

Then flipping her pad back to the first page with a smile she added PASSION next to the P in Sparkle enjoying the feeling of filling this in and even the warmth of her Nan's presence.

P = Passion

She enjoyed a mouthful of hot sweet tea whilst thinking that if this word Sparkle was to be her guiding principle for success what other key factors would help her achieve her true aspirations?

Putting her previous experiences in life and business to one side she allowed her imagination to run wild. Following her desires to where she wanted to be a year from now, five years, maybe even 10, she affirmed to herself there are no limits.

This mental path seemed a little hazy at first but as she started to put the words down it made some sense.

'The way home was inside you all the time' Isn't that what the Good Witch says in *The Wizard of Oz?* I need to sparkle up my ruby slippers!

Gemma desired:

- Her own business again, this time on her terms.
- Financial freedom.
- A beautiful holiday home cum permanent home.
- A long loving relationship with Ryan.
- Loving, confident, well educated children and to always stay emotionally close to them.
- To travel the world in style.
- To help others achieve a better quality of life.

Suddenly she felt a little selfish as to why she should have it all when there was so much suffering and unhappiness in the world? Who was she to think so big and have such grand ideas? Surely she has enough already?

Gemma reasoned to herself that if there was nothing more to do then she wouldn't have these desires. That her intentions towards others were good, her dreams honourable and by being in a better financial position she would stand to help others more.

Gemma could live with that concept and inspired wrote large across the page:

*It's better to spend money like there's no tomorrow than to spend tonight like there's no hope!*

I'm sure that's an old Irish saying...anyway... Okay, she thought to herself as she felt she had exhausted her list of desires, now I'm at the top of my game I am successful and have financial control over my life. I enjoy my life and my money. My success benefits others. Now, looking back what qualities did it take to get here?

Gemma thought long and hard before scribbling: 'It wasn't through sitting on my backside getting fatter whilst life passed me by.'

That's if I could get any fatter at the moment!' she grumbled.

Starting writing again as if she had already achieved her plans she added;

> My goals were reached by continuously moving forward and taking action, building relationships, using my intuition and knowledge. By trusting and loving those who worked with me and valuing those who wanted our services. I maintained my momentum and kept the enthusiasm and passion flowing constantly.

She was enjoying herself this morning and didn't want the flow to stop. Reviewing her notes she quickly circled several words from her last paragraph and with a grin from ear to ear filled in the missing words to her acronym.

S = ~~Simple~~ Simplicity

P = Passion

A = Action

R = Relationships

K = ~~Knowledge~~ Knowing?

L = Love

E = Enthusiasm

This was Gemma's eureka moment. This would help guide and inspire her. Gemma wanted to shout out to the world and let them share her little secret.

In her heart Gemma knew most people would not want to listen.

She knew that the majority of people would rather take their music to their graves, many paralysed by fear. Fear of trying something new. Fear of failure with all its repercussions. Fear of being different. In many people's minds these fears easily outweighed the potential rewards of success.

Gemma's thoughts turned to her best friend Pauline who had died, at the age of 41, from cancer. Pauline had wanted to do so much with her life but there had never been the right time to start.

'You'll never plough a field by turning it over in your mind.'

Gemma thought she heard her Nan talking. The words spinning around her head certainly had an Irish lilt to them.

'Good thing I don't believe in ghosts.' Gemma said, 'though… if I did I could let Pauline know how well her children are doing and how much I miss her.'

She switched her laptop on and hurriedly sent an email to her former colleague Hilary; determined to try something different as soon as possible. You never know what fate may have in store.

## 3. One small Step For Woman, But One Giant Leap For (Man)kind!

# Life SPARKLES

*Inaction breeds doubt and fear.
Action breeds confidence and courage.*

*If you want to conquer fear do not
sit at home and think about it.*

*Go out and get busy.*
Dale Carnegie

After getting the kids ready for school and dropping them off, picking up Ryan's shirts from the dry cleaners, popping into the supermarket for a few little bits and finishing off some light housework Gemma finally settled into her favourite armchair and put her feet up.

She had finished work on Friday, promising colleagues to return next year, but Gemma was set on a steady course to ensure that was one promise she would be forced to break.

Earlier she had received a call from Hilary. They had been in regular e-mail contact but the time had come to take things up a notch. Hilary wanted to see if Gemma was free for lunch to discuss this new idea of hers and this was one meeting not to be postponed.

Hilary, a good friend and confidante, was someone Gemma trusted. She knew her opinion and input would be a great boost. She also knew Hilary wouldn't hold back if she felt something wasn't quite right. Gemma prepared for her arrival by writing a short action plan with several headings and pointers.

They had originally met working at BG&R years ago, where Hilary had also been a casualty of the old firm's macho attitude. She wasn't a mother, but equally wasn't part of the Old Boy network and was only too pleased to throw off the power suit and join Gemma's crusade.

Hilary hadn't worked since the collapse of Gemma's business. Though she was more than able to get another job she chose to do a little volunteer work for a local hospice to keep busy instead. She was in her early 50s with the trim figure of someone 20 years younger, always impeccably dressed with a chic and classic style. It was this natural deportment which undoubtedly secured the hand of her equally immaculate, silver-haired husband James Buchanan, QC.

Together they had worked to build his law practice and Hilary was now able to enjoy the benefits of a healthy investment portfolio, a home with no mortgage and no children.

'Never wanted them, sweetie. Love other people's – like your two – absolutely darling, but I'm not maternal. It's not for me.'

Ryan always joked it was like speaking to Hyacinth Bucket from *Keeping Up Appearances* except that, unlike Hyacinth, Hilary was one of the kindest and most sincere people you could ever wish to meet. For Gemma she was a perfect choice to push the business idea further.

'I simply love the idea,' exclaimed Hilary crisply.

Hilary's property knowledge and genuine love of people could always win anyone over. And, as she didn't operate from a place of need, she could usually be counted on to focus on the vision. However, within seconds of loving the idea reality reared its ugly head,

'But you do not have the start-up capital to reinvent the property portal market. As we all know Rightmove have that pretty much sown up.'

'I know,' responded Gemma, 'we are not going to fight fire with fire; we are going to be the flea on the cash cow's back!'

'I don't think I like the idea of being thought of as a flea,' Hilary laughed.

'I've read a lot lately and time and time again I come across networking being the future,' Gemma responded and without giving Hilary the chance to reply she added, 'I have also done a lot of soul searching and looking at things with fresh eyes. I am convinced together we could create a niche vehicle for estate agents of the future. Give those that work for us the opportunity to build their own little business within a business; with excellent financial incentives, support and training; whilst giving home owners the chance to sell their homes without exorbitant costs.'

'Sounds divine... in an ideal world darling.'

'We all know there is no such thing,' Gemma retorted, 'there is always some git trying to put a spoke in your wheel. But this time we are all wiser. And we have a vision. There will be minimal start up costs. Initially we can work from home; the training can happen on line or over the phone. All I do know is that it can be done.'

She passed Hilary her A4 pad opened to the first page. After reviewing it a little smile appeared on her flawless complexion.

'That is wonderful,' she smiled.

'How and when do you want to get going? Sometime in the spring when the baby is a little older?'

'No I can't wait that long, I want to get going immediately. Of course I will have my hands full very shortly, but, we need to carry out some extra research and test our ideas. Then we need to get a new web mistress; someone who knows about networking programmes. We can also have some fun choosing a name and register a domain etc. Next we find 15,000 business partners and ensure they're trained to our charter and then we...'

Okay darling,' Hilary interrupted. 'You haven't changed have you? Still a veritable fireball of ideas. Let's get one thing done at a time. I will e-mail you some ideas on strategy and then get in touch with my nephew. He has started to work for a web design and marketing company. Though I fancy he will dislike the label 'mistress' but who knows? I'll put out some feelers. You have a rest. Speak later.'

Gemma was ecstatic that Hilary was with her. She had vision, ideas and the ability to get others to see her views, but she always struggled with the implementation. Hilary's strength lay in her administrative and organisational skills. It would be great when they started to earn money, but more than the financial rewards, Gemma wanted the feeling of making a positive difference to the lives of others again.

Gemma hadn't realised quite how much she had missed her clients and the joy of finding others their perfect home. It was the satisfaction of making people's dreams come true and the sweet joy of handing over the keys to a new family that really inspired her. And she knew Hilary's passion lay here too.

Together, Gemma knew they could create a haven for jaded estate agents and anxious house hunters, where agents, buyers and vendors could live in harmony, an virtual oasis in the property desert ...

With all this dancing round her fertile mind Gemma let herself drift off to sleep, in the comfort of her armchair, feeling as if finally she could achieve something very special.

***

The Coven finally met at Vino's Wine Bar – the original, if rather tired, 1980s yuppie paradise they use to stake out when they were all at university.

'Can you believe this place is still here?'

'And it hasn't changed one bit. Doesn't that waiter look like Rick Astley?'

'It probably is Rick Astley. *Never gonna give you up, never gonna let you down.*'

'Ah, memories. Do you remember watching the video screen in the corner over there? What was that song that was number one forever...from *The Bodyguard*?'

'Ah yes, I remember you had a thing for Kevin Costner!'

'Yeah, he's probably got a job here too!'

The Coven was back. It had been too long. Increasingly Gemma was becoming aware how important good relationships were. One shouldn't let friendships fade away.

Tulip was the artist of the group. Just before her 21st birthday she had decided to change her name and her course, abandoning law for design, and never looked back. Now a highly successful graphic designer she thought Gemma's desire to give setting up on her own another try was 'Stupendous! I've always done my own thing, followed my bliss, you know. Hasn't done me any harm.'

'But you don't have a family,' piped up Siobhan. 'You are very brave and having another baby too. *Three* children, Gemma. I struggle with Tyler – but then he's a sensitive child. I would love to go back to work now he's at school but he's so fragile and often unwell. I need to be at home. He needs to know Mummy is there for him. And, well, maybe in a few years I'll get a little job locally; before my brain freezes over!'

'Siobhan, how do you stay sane?' Toni (short for Antonia) asked. Toni asked this question of all her friends who stayed at home with their children, even if it was for an afternoon! For Toni the idea of not having a career was abhorrent. She had worked hard to get where she was, and where she was was pretty remarkable. Chief Executive of a national aid charity, constantly in demand for radio and television debates, famous blogger and author she was 'having it all' - except her 'all' did not include kids or a husband, or even a boyfriend.

'So, Gemma – when is this. Ryan, going to make an honest women of you?' Sophie asked.

Sophie, like Siobhan, was married with kids but she had not stopped working when the children came along. Instead she had downsized her ambition, gone part time and adjusted her work to get it all done before she needed to pick up the twins from school.

'Surely, you are not going to make that mistake again!' shrieked Toni. 'Why do all of you still insist that you need a man to 'complete you' ?'

'I blame Jerry McGuire, personally,' choked Siobhan as she sipped her Vodka and Red Bull.

'No, Rene Zellweger and bloody Bridget Jones!' trumpeted Tulip, slamming her glass on to the table.

'Yes, bloody Bridget Jones, I mean how could you even consider Hugh Grant over Mr Darcy?'

'Ryan has a look of Colin Firth actually, Sophie, with the body of Colin Farrell. And I'm not making the same mistake twice; Toni. Ryan is nothing like Rob. Nothing at all.'

'Thank God for that,' they all agreed. 'Here's to Gemma, and new beginnings!'

'Yes, new beginnings!' toasted Gemma.

Over the next week Gemma, Hilary and Ryan tossed ideas back and forth and spent endless hours trawling the internet for the bigger picture; gaining greater insights into the way things could be improved.

After their initial research Team Oasis (as they had started to call themselves) put together an action plan and check-list. Hilary had the idea of contacting the National Association of Estate Agents; as she was still a member she felt they would pass on contact details of those who were in the process of closing down. After all, they would have nothing to lose in trying new ideas and they would already be established in their communities and might still have listings.

Gemma worked on a business and marketing plan.

She also made the first tentative calls to banks and to an old business friend who ran a radio PR company. Clive had previously managed to get her some airtime on the local radio to discuss 'the true value of your home today', which had been fun, and whetted her appetite to do more. Clive was confident that with the right timing this story could be huge and even be of interest to the national radio stations.

Gemma's confidence was overflowing. She was also enjoying the latter stages of her pregnancy and had been complimented on several occasions over the past week on how radiant she looked. Though it would take a giant puppeteer working her legs with a bungee rope to put a spring in her step at the moment, it did make her feel wonderful.

Gemma had now started reviewing her notes a little later in the day, but still managed time to meditate before everyone was up in the morning.

This time she didn't want to put a foot wrong and so stuck to her now familiar routine as best she could.

Ryan accused her of being a control freak but Gemma found it unnatural to retain this level of focus and discipline, it took a lot of effort. She had always been creative. Even as a young girl she would be busy organising her friends into dance routines or drawing pictures for the school fête. Ideas were second nature, and she was often accused of being the dreamer of the family. This time she was determined the dreams would become reality and that the execution of her business plan would be as close to perfect as possible. No detail would be ignored, there would be no short cuts and she would find a way around every obstacle. Like the Bear Hunt story she read the kids at bedtime 'if we can't go over it and we can't go under it - we'll have to go through it!

Hilary moved into the next stages of her action plan and started calling prospective estate agents within a 30-mile radius of their original working area. She set aside two hours in the morning and two hours in the late afternoon and recorded every detail of the calls for feedback to Gemma.

After three lacklustre days of cold calling with responses ranging from 'You cannot be serious!' to 'Things will improve soon so we don't have to change anything' Hilary was concerned about relaying her lack of success back to Gemma when she called.

'I feel like an early mammal overhearing the last two dinosaurs chatting by a frozen lake, 'Don't worry everything's going to be Okay it's a light frost!' Hilary joked.

'Exactly,' Gemma chortled, 'we are heralding in the dawn of a new 'Nice' age!'

'That is awful. Sweetie, do not give up the day job.'

'I have no plans to – it's too much fun!'

After their call Gemma sent a quick e-mail over to reaffirm the conversation:

> To: Hilary@cheapbroadband.net
>
> Subject: Keep going Hilary; it's a matter of time.
>
> I know you taught me most of the stuff below, but it never hurts to hear it again, even from your favourite student. :-)
>
> REMEMBER SPARKLE!
>
> - Don't over sell yourself.
> - Listen.
> - Focus on the benefits to the listener.
> - This is not for everyone.
> - Don't take it personally.
> - Smile, smile, smile.
> - And if there is still no rapport, don't talk no more!
>
> Love
>
> Gems x

This lifted Hilary's spirits and the next day on the seventh call she made a breakthrough. It was with a husband and wife team who had a chain of three estate agents only an hour's drive away. She made an appointment to meet them. Then, as if by magic, Hilary arranged a further five appointments by the end of the day.

The snowball had been set in motion.

## 4: Mamma Mia!

# Life SPA_R_KLES

*We must put back into society what we have taken out. And if we don't love our staff, our neighbours, the environment, we'll all be doomed. I want to make it attractive to be good.*
Dame Anita Roddick

The next week flew by for Gemma; there was so much to do before the baby came and Hilary was constantly on the phone with progress reports and new issues that needed immediate attention.

Jayne was around more, which was great. Gemma was itching to discuss her plans with her but bit her tongue. She knew her sister's response would have been well meant but she would concentrate only on the practicalities. Unfortunately, this meant that Gemma had to keep her ideas secret from her mother as well. Though her Mum was always cheery, a well-intentioned but doubtful word from her at this point would have dented Gemma's faith in the future. Whilst she knew one has to be realistic (something she had learnt the hard way) she also knew criticism from someone you love could spell disaster at the early stages of a project. She decided she would wait until they had their first earning Associate (this was the new term booted around at the moment within Team Oasis).

With only four weeks before the baby was due Gemma felt an urgency quite unlike anything she had experienced before. Every minute counted and it was a struggle balancing her passion to get on with her business plans and maintaining any semblance of family life. Yes, physically she was more tired but she knew that things would be much worse after the birth. A new baby is a wonderful gift in any home but sleepless nights, nursing and nappy changing whilst juggling the older kids' timetables and simply running the home would take its toll. Gemma knew that she had to get the groundwork completed now.

Already there were signs of strain. Ryan had started to take some afternoons away from work to spend more time with the family; helping with school runs and the like. He insisted that Gemma made the most of the offers of help from her family and friends and rest. But Gemma took every opportunity to work instead.

With Ryan a member of the Team, and one of the few people Gemma felt safe to discuss the business with, even their downtime revolved around work.

He appeared to be an never-ending source of support and love but in her heart Gemma knew their priorities were changing and she needed to balance her work and her life. Especially her love life.

This is Ryan's first child, she reminded herself. He is nervous and scared and overwhelmed with anticipation. And he's right. I must look after my health and my sanity but...

Gemma had long known how critical it is to develop strong and mutually beneficial relationships in business and life in general. No one can achieve anything worthwhile without the co-operation of others. Though previously she had put her trust in the wrong people, she now felt comfortable sharing her hopes and desires with Ryan and appreciated how much he had boosted her self-confidence and self-esteem.

I don't want the business to get in the way of all this, she thought, and yet I am already keeping secrets from my Mum and sister.

It's timing. I will tell them and I don't need to feel guilty about not sharing yet. But. I also need to build a strong network and not rely on one or two people. I need Ryan's support but I mustn't abuse it.

Gemma considered how her organisational model depended on networking – creating a circle of business Friends and Family. Everyone helps each other. We use the skills, knowledge and experience of the group. But it means give and take. All relationships – business or personal – need to be nurtured & cultivated. Even those in my personal life! Gemma mused.

Watching her father building up his construction company proved to be a valuable lesson in leadership skills. Gemma loved the way her Dad always managed to juggle contractors, the bank manager, about 30 employees plus the accountant and the tax man and always with a smile on his face. But, unfortunately, he began leaving more of the day-to-day running to his younger partners and started playing more golf. He didn't see the cracks appearing, and about six months later was out of business.

The same thing happened to Gemma when she took her eye off the ball. Now it was time to learn from the lessons of the past. Back then she gave all she had and demanded nothing in return; now she could see she was in danger of doing the complete opposite.

Christmas was a few weeks away and Gemma suddenly had a terrible thought: What's the date?

Checking her diary she could see that Sam's school nativity concert was that afternoon!

What's the time now? 1.30 already? The concert starts in 30 minutes!

She threw on her coat and frantically searched for her scarf and gloves.

Pulling open the utility room door she spied Katie's shepherd outfit hanging on the rack.

Oh no! They have a dress rehearsal today don't they?. Thank God I saw it – I can pop it in to her class on the way. What is wrong with my brain?

Squeezing herself behind the wheel of the car Gemma tried taking some deep breaths to calm herself down. The last thing I need is to go into labour during *Hark the herald angels sing*, she thought.

Remembering the mantra she had read, in one of the many books she had devoured over the past few months, Gemma started to repeat to herself out loud,

'I accept I am experiencing frustration, and that's okay. I am willing to consider I am a great mother and my life is in perfect order. I feel calm, right now.'

Along with deep breathing this seemed to help. After a few minutes, composure regained, Gemma set off to enjoy the concert.

About 4.30pm Gemma made a quick call to Hilary and another to Karl, their new web designer, who was looking to have a site up and running by the end of January. Then, with Katie and Sam (fortified with milk and toast smothered in Nutella) happily creating Christmas cards for their grandparents at the kitchen table, Gemma turned her attention to her A4 pad...

## Relationships

Do unto others as you would have others do unto you.

For our very survival as a company we must develop strong lasting relationships, with both our Associates and our customers.

For our very survival as a family we must develop strong lasting relationships! How?

- Take the time
- Listen
- Keep promises
- Say thank you
- Accept responsibility
- Don't blame
- Value people as individuals
- Give and take – keep things in balance!
- Think of the kids school motto - 'We are all different, we are all equal' - when dealing with difficult people!

Gemma hesitated before writing again, thinking about the women in her life. Gemma often thought about her Nan but rarely considered her Nonni (her mother's mother). Probably because she was so far away in Italy and yet her presence was clear in everything Gemma's Mum said and did. Both tirelessly looked after their respective families, constantly cooking, cleaning, mending and smiling all the while. Never, ever appearing stressed out at all. Both always appearing effortlessly beautiful.

There is much I need to learn from them. They would never have forgotten a school play. They always had time for each and every member of the family.

Making meatballs with Nonni is one of my best memories. There was no rush. Pavarotti serenaded us as Nonni, Jayne and I mixed the beef, spices and flour. My aunt was in charge of the pasta and

Mamma stirred the home-made tomato sauce. No Dolmio or Ragu here. Ah, the aroma. My cousins, Giuseppe and Claudio, were commissioned with finding fresh herbs from the garden and the menfolk made the salad and poured the drinks. There was an energy, a passion, constant chat and laughter, but no one swore or shouted at each other. There was always order and respect.

- Break up and assign tasks.
- Prioritising is key to success.
- It's all in the detail.
- Good manners cost nothing!

'It's all interconnected!' Gemma concluded.

'Of course,' she mumbled, 'that has been the key to every relationship in the world since the dawn of time. We have all become too self obsessed and selfish in our daily lives, expecting to receive more than we give.'

She had always hated politicians using such phrases as 'It's time for some good old fashioned values' but perhaps there was something to it after all.

But not in the way they mean. Unity and respect and good manners – we have lost them somewhere. Women should not be tied to the kitchen sink. We need to fulfil our dreams and potential by doing what we do best (whatever that may be). But to do that we have to make time work for us. We need to value the contribution of others and delegate more efficiently.

- Having it all doesn't mean doing it all!
- Take help from others with more time or stronger skills in that area.
- Use the knowledge and expertise of others wisely
- Do the right thing at the right time!

And…

Gemma remembered an old cross stitch picture hanging in the spare room. It had been made by her Nan when she was a child back in Ireland.

*Take the time to work,
for it is the price of success.*

*Take the time to think,
it is the source of strength.*

*Take the time to play,
it is the secret of youth.*

*Take the time to read,
it is the seed of wisdom.*

*Take the time to be friendly,
for it brings happiness.*

*Take the time to dream,
for it will carry you to the stars.*

*Take the time to love,
it is the joy of life.*

*Take the time to be content,
it is the music of the soul.*

'Perfect,' exclaimed Gemma as she took the picture off the wall to move it to a more prominent place. Then the phone rang; it was her mother.

'*Ciao bella*! How was Sam's concert? Sorry I couldn't get off work to see it but I'm looking forward to Katie's play – tomorrow at seven isn't it?'

'*Ciao Mamma*, Sam was a star, of course. Don't tell but I almost missed the concert. It completely went out of my head. Remembered in time. Of course there were no seats when I got there so I had to stand at the back but he saw me when he came in. My back is killing me now though. I feel so stupid. How could I forget? Must be the pregnancy. '

'Bella, there is an old Italian saying which goes like this: *La gatta frettolosa fece i gatini ciechi.* Or in English - the hurried cat produced blind kittens. You must learn to get things in order so you can relax. Everything has its time. I am always here you know. You do not need to do everything on your own. That's what others are here for.'

'I know Mamma, I am beginning to realise that.'

## 5: Let It Be

# Life SPAR<u>K</u>LES

*Be like the bird that pausing in her flight,*
*While on boughs too slight*
*Feels them give way beneath her and yet sings*
*Knowing she has wings.*
Victor Hugo

Gemma had been staring blankly at her pad for nearly 15 minutes.

She was trying to focus on the K in SPARKLE. Up to now she had found the whole process enlightening and it was proving to be more than a formula for her new business, it was turning into the blueprint of how she wished to spend the rest of her life. Gemma was determined her diaries would not gather dust, with her old keepsakes, but stay in constant view and be kept updated. She would persevere even on bad hair days and when her confidence was low; even more so on days like that.

It had been months since Gemma first wrote the words against her SPARKLE acronym and they had flowed instinctively, but, somehow the word Knowing was causing her problems.

Why use knowing? Was it a whim so that it fitted in my little acronym? After all what do I know about knowing? I didn't know my business was going down the pan until it was too late. I didn't know that rat of a first husband was cheating on me. Except looking back I think I did. Little niggles telling me things weren't right? I talked myself out of it. My head told me to get over it and keep going. She had a sip of water.

Maybe, maybe, it was self-denial? I had known all along but wasn't prepared to listen to my heart and my own inner being. Perhaps I was afraid? Maybe I was afraid that I would be right and couldn't face the pain of separation or knowing the truth? Or the thought of being a failure? I believed in true love and marriage for life – these suspicions simply did not fit into my belief system so I ignored them?

Gemma picked her pen back up and under Notes of the Day quickly scrawled...

> Having trouble focusing on the word knowing,
> will get back when I know!

She laughed at herself and thought: If that's not a contradiction I don't know what is.

Closing her pad Gemma went to prepare a light lunch for Ryan as he was due home shortly. Through the rest of the day she kept the word 'knowing' at the forefront of her mind waiting for a little inspiration to surface. Eventually she went to bed and decided to let it go... for now.

Wriggling under Ryan's heavy arm Gemma gently slid out of bed. Without disturbing him she put her dressing gown on and headed downstairs. Switching on the kitchen light she saw it had turned 4.30am! She felt like she had been awake all night. The baby had been playing football in her belly. Mother Nature's way of preparing her for the sleepless nights to come? Her thoughts returned to Ryan snoring; someone was in for a sharp wakeup call!

Dimming the kitchen lights she settled into one of the high backed oak chairs around the table. The strength and rigidity of the wood was comforting. It made her feel supported physically and mentally. Preparing herself to meditate she set the alarm on her phone and placed a cushion behind her back. Gently closing her eyes she followed her usual pattern of deep breathing and feeling, what Gemma could only describe as bliss as the energy circulated her tired body. She even felt the baby settle, and though maybe her imagination, she could sense it going through a similar process. Gemma smiled to herself and drifted off into her own little world.

All too soon Enrique woke her again from her alternative universe. Gemma reached across the table for her diary and laptop. She quickly jotted down her normal format; working through her intentions for the day.

It was now virtually impossible to start the day without this morning routine.

She checked her e-mails.

At the insistence of Ryan and Hilary she tried not to worry about the new business and to focus her attention on resting for the two weeks before the birth, but couldn't resist checking her e-mails at least twice a day and making the odd note.

Even between buying a few late Christmas gifts for Sam and Katie online she would get sidetracked and start surfing the internet for ideas or checking out the competition. It had been most productive as she gleaned valuable insights into self-employed estate agents, affiliate networking, online marketing and so on. She even ventured as far afield as the USA and Australia; copying and pasting little titbits into her ideas folder.

Gemma had also become a fan of Facebook. She had read that it was a useful online tool and knew that such social networking sites should be used for business, but it was becoming very addictive, especially the quizzes: What kind of handbag would you be? Can you name these cartoon characters? Do you know your onions? etc. and she hadn't begun to explore Twitter yet!

After 15 minutes on the laptop she turned back to her diary and under Notes for the Day and, once again, wrote:

Knowing

Though she had had no flashes of brilliance over the last 16 hours she felt at ease within herself, accepting that something would come if she didn't push too hard. She reread the lines she had scrawled:

> No one knows everything and what we believe we *do* know is a reflection of our own values and experiences of life.
>
> Many of our beliefs are passed down from generation to generation, from spouses, friends, school, the media or society (sometimes holding us back from achieving anything worthwhile with our lives).

Exactly, she thought. If someone tells you day after day how useless you are then it's bound to affect you eventually. You start believing that you can't amount to much in life, and as I now know, the more you focus on something the more of it you get back. Wow, everything seems to return to the Law of Attraction. Maybe Dad's books do make sense and it's the natural order of life.

- I blocked out my own inner being for so long!
- I have lacked confidence.
- Suffered low self-esteem.
- I had completely forgotten the ability to listen to ME.

All of the positive love and praise I received as a kid was all undone within eight years of living with someone who, for want of a better word, mentally abused me. Maybe the little success I did achieve was brought on from my upbringing but eventually it was suffocated by my own and others' negativity.

SO?

Does this have anything to do with knowing?

Gemma answered her own question without a pause, 'Maybe Knowing is a combination of so many things it's hard to define. Yes of course it is. She continued to note:

> I have the ability to choose my own thoughts and accept responsibility for the rest of my life.
>
> The answers I need as I go through life are within me.
>
> All I have to do is listen to my gut instincts and
>
> Believe in MYSELF a lot more!
>
> Of course I don't know everything and never will. This isn't about knowledge; it's about knowing.
>
> When I require Knowledge I'll get others' opinions and advice on subjects I am ignorant about. That's different to going along with other people's beliefs – doing what they think is right for me. Only I can know that. At the end of the day I am responsible for my life.
>
> And in areas where I am accountable, like my children's welfare. I must do what I think is right, in that moment, but they, ultimately, are the only ones who know what is right for them. I will listen and do my best to polish their individual SPARKLES!
>
> I can develop a greater self-belief if I can trust my own decisions more. The only way to do that is by practising making more and more decisions. My decisions need to be informed. I need to listen and then allow the right answer to come to me.

Nodding she vaguely recalled a saying her Dad had about keeping an open mind. Now what was that? Something about parasols? Umbrellas? No, I remember.

> *The mind is like a parachute,*
> *it only works when it is open.*

Gemma was feeling pleased with herself and the constant tiredness had subsided briefly. She knew it would only be for a short while, but somehow these early morning 'me time' sessions always seemed so meaningful. The simple things in life really are the most precious.

Gemma eased herself out of the chair and went to the sink to get a glass of water. Though not her usual habit, for fear of waking everyone else up, Gemma reached over and switched on the radio. The dying notes of Queen's *Don't stop me now* entered the room, followed by the unnaturally chirpy DJ announcing 'Well, my fellow night owls, or maybe you're early birds? One thing's for sure it's always a good time for. The Beatles *and Let it Be!*'

As Gemma sat back down to her journal Paul McCartney's voice wrapped around her like the mist off the Mull of Kintyre.

*When I find myself in times of trouble*

*Mother Mary comes to me*

*Speaking words of wisdom*

*Let it be.*

*And in my hour of darkness she is*

*standing right in front of me*

*Speaking words of wisdom,*

*Let it be.*

A warm, fuzzy feeling washed over Gemma. As the song continued Gemma reflected on her life over the past few months. She had come a long way, but it wasn't all about learning something new; it was as much about looking at many things she had always known in a fresh light. She felt that finally she was actually understanding and grasping the concepts contained in her father's books. But, more than that, she was beginning to realise that the greatest lessons were coming from sources much closer to home.

Gemma was appreciating all her experiences and understood the wisdom of her own heart. Is that something that comes with age? Seems that reading all these books Dad no more had the answers than my mother who shunned them! Yet they were both so wise. And my grandmothers too. Without the advantage of all these so-called experts and learned journals they had an inner knowing that made the impossible possible.

*When all the broken hearted*
*people living in the world agree*

*There will be an answer*

*Let it be.*

She recalled having said to Ryan, a couple of weeks earlier, that if she had realised she knew all of this before she would have never made the mistakes she had. He gently reminded her that without mistakes in the past how would she understand when she knew and when she didn't? All our experiences teach us valuable lessons. Without them she wouldn't be as mentally strong, and as sexy, as she was now! He also went on to say that life isn't designed to be perfect all of the time. How boring it would be if it were? It was the natural ebb and flow of life, and when it was flowing for her go with it because she deserved it.

*and when the night is cloudy,*

*there is still a light that shines on me*

Gemma turned to a fresh page.

*Speaking words of wisdom*

*Let it be.*

*Let it be, Let it be, Let it be, oh Let it be*

## Developing Knowing

- Make decisions – and listen to how I feel... I'll start to know what's right and wrong.
- Mistakes are feedback. Learn from them and move on.
- Ask, ask, ask until I get a gut instinct.
- Learn something from everyone I meet; both the positive and negative aspects of their personalities can be useful.
- Listen to my own inner being; the answers are always within me.
- Don't be afraid to make bold decisions.
- Don't spend the rest of my life following the herd; become a shepherd.

Gemma loved the analogy of being a shepherd and leading her flock through the trials and tribulations of life. What psalm is it? The Lord is my shepherd; I shall not want. He makes me lie down in green pastures, he leads me beside still waters, he restores my soul.

Actually is that what knowing is all about? Trusting the God within us. That voice that keeps telling us a course of action is right or wrong? Mother Mary speaking words of wisdom. Wow!

That knowing we feel in our hearts is always right; we must follow it regardless of what the chatter outside or inside our heads is telling us. Trust your inner wisdom, your God voice and your cup will runneth over!

*Remember always to trust your own heart. Everything will be fine. SPARKLE!*

In her heart Gemma suddenly felt that she had a greater understanding than ever before. She could really help others succeed and was on the right path to do so.

Closing her pad Gemma thought of Ryan upstairs; she might grab a cuddle before the kids woke up.

# 6: A Chocolate & Duvet Day!

# Life SPARK_LES

*Everyone of us gets through the tough times because somebody is there standing in the gap to close it for us.*

**Oprah Winfrey**

'It's a bonny baby girl. Are you the father?'

Ryan gently nodded and the bubbly midwife handed him a little warm bundle in a pink shawl.

'Now, can I trust you with this little mite whilst we see to Mother?'

'Of course. She will be okay?' Ryan whispered afraid to hear the answer.

'Sure me darling. Caesareans are very common. You can come back in in a little while – she took us all by surprise, that's all.'

The baby was healthy but there had been complications and Gemma had been rushed into theatre. There had been no time for him to scrub up to go with her, so he had to stay outside, feeling helpless.

Holding his precious daughter Ryan felt totally helpless. He had promised Gemma to always be there and yet, in the end, she went through this alone.

Looking at his daughter Ryan's eyes filled with tears of joy whilst in his heart raged a clawing anxiety for the health of his best friend and the woman he loved.

Having lost her for nearly 20 years, he wasn't ready to lose her again.

He held the baby close to him relishing her perfect features and revelling in the scent of her fresh skin. He whispered to her about the fun they were all going to have as a family, and about all the places in the world they were going to visit, but most of all that he would always be there for her.

Gemma could feel the presence of someone in the room.

As she tried hard to focus she saw a familiar outline standing by her bed. Smiling, her Nan leant over her and gently kissed her forehead and in a soft lilting voice murmured 'Not yet darling.'

Gemma felt a strange warmth envelope her whole body, causing her to wake with a start. As she did she saw Ryan's adoring yet relieved blue eyes,

'Sorry didn't want to make you jump; I had to kiss you.'

Tenderly sweeping a wisp of her hair from the side of her face he leant over her and kissed her gently, on the lips.

'I've missed you; don't do that to me again.'

Gemma smiled back and whispered, 'I don't plan to!'

Gemma didn't mention the vision. Perhaps she might have if she had realised how serious her condition had been. She felt it had been a lovely dream and, as she had been thinking so much of the wise old lady, it wasn't really all that odd.

*I gliobach í an cherc go dtógann sí a hāl.*

*The hen has ruffled feathers
until she rears her brood.*
Irish Gaelic saying

The days were drifting into weeks and the weeks soon turned into months – two in fact - before Gemma was back in touch with reality.

The notebook, the daily meditations and her desires to start a new business were from a previous life, now almost forgotten. Hilary had been in touch several times – more to see how she and the baby were doing than to ask about progress on the business – and that was fine.

Gemma had more than enough to cope with as baby Holly had a set mantra of 'Feed me now or I'll cry and cry.'

'Perhaps we should have named you Violet Elizabeth I'll scweam and scweam and scweam until I'm sick!' joked Gemma, although she wasn't finding the experience at all funny. Once fed, Holly would have trouble winding and then cry for another hour before nodding off, only to be disturbed by a creaky door or floorboard or a fly landing on the branch of the willow tree next door!

Gemma felt she was neglecting Sam and Katie. Though they loved their baby sister it was amusing, and slightly worrying, to overhear Sam sigh on returning from school one day, 'Oh, is Holly still here? I thought Mum would have taken her back by now!'

'This is meant to be one of the happiest times of my life! I'm sure I was okay with Sam and Katie straight away,' she grumbled at her reflection, noting the bags forming under her eyes. She hardly recognised herself; her hair was tousled, her skin pale, and several spots were appearing on her chin to add to her misery. Some size zero soap star was pushing her new workout video on *This Morning* in the background and Gemma felt physically sick at her evangelical conviction about the wonders of pelvic floor exercises and post natal sex.

Looking down at her bulging belly, hidden under Ryan's England rugby sweatshirt and grey jogging bottoms, intimacy of any description was the last thing on Gemma's mind. Though Ryan was a very patient man there would only be so much of an icy atmosphere he could take.

Gemma tried to be her amorous old self but this hormonal roller coaster was distancing her from the love of her life.

Holly had settled for a much-needed nap and, wanting a little comfort herself, Gemma grabbed the duvet off of her bed and headed downstairs to watch an old film and have a little chocolate. If a whole bar of family-sized Chocofest (made for sharing) could be described as little that is - though this was merely a light snack these days.

As she reached into the cupboard Gemma glimpsed her diary sitting on the dresser out of the corner of her eye.

'That's odd. I'm sure it was on the other side yesterday,' she mumbled, then looking closer saw a piece of paper sticking out of it. Curious, she took the diary with the chocolate into the front room. Choosing *Dirty Dancing* to watch, from her Guilty Pleasures DVD collection, Gemma pulled the duvet over her and tried to rest the best she could. But the diary kept calling to her and, despite the efforts of Patrick Swayze to distract her, after 10 minutes or so Gemma picked her diary up and opened it to where the sheet of paper lay.

Hi Darling

Found it easier to write than to say, but I wanted to let you know that I love you, and our beautiful family. I am so proud of you. You are amazing.

I also wanted to say that I will always stand by you whatever you choose to do with your life, but please reread your notes before you give up on your dreams. Maybe you are not ready right now but I don't want you to have any regrets when we are old and grey.

Love always.

Ryan x

Emotional blackmail eh? God I love him, but I hate him too – I've just had a baby for heaven's sake! I'm not superwoman, or Wonder Woman, in fact, right now I'm more like the cat lady off the Simpsons!

Gemma thumped the cushion beside her, pushed it up to her face and sobbed hysterically.

When there were no more tears left to cry, she peeled the soggy cushion away and wiped her face with a tissue.

Chocolate! she thought as she reached for the bar.

Gemma couldn't bring herself to look at her Golden Notebook but instead rested her head back on the cushion and pulled the duvet up to her chin. 'No one puts Baby in a corner,' she chanted as she drifted off to sleep.

A soul-shredding high pitched wail over the remote from little Holly woke Gemma. She was convinced that if Holly had been born first she would have remained an only child ... who spent a lot of time with her grandparents! Turning the sound down on the intercom Gemma grabbed the phone. After five rings it was answered.

'Hi Mamma it's only me, when will you be around next?'

Within the hour there was the rattling of keys in the front door and footsteps up the hallway.

'*Ciao bella*, came as quickly as I could. Is everything okay?'

Gemma's mother bent down and kissed her on the forehead, reaching to take Holly from her lap. After five minutes of cooing and doesn't she look like me gestures she returned her attention to her daughter.

Not wishing to spoil the moment Gemma bit her tongue but mused that Holly looked nothing like her mother. Holly was a sweet strawberry blonde, with blue eyes and a little pug nose, whilst her mother was brunette, and had green almond eyes with strong Roman features. But looking at her mother, as the late afternoon winter sun filtered through the window illuminating her olive skin, Gemma realised how beautiful she really was, and, though she didn't resemble Holly in the slightest, she could easily give Sophia Loren a run for her money.

Now 62, she would still turn men's heads. When she was younger Gemma would feel embarrassed by the attention she attracted, and no matter how young or old, handsome or repulsive her admirers, her mother would wink at her and say *In amore tutti gli uomini sono stati creati uguali* (Love makes all men equal).

'I can remember how hard it is these first few months darling; Jayne was an absolute nightmare! I don't think I spoke to your papa for three months and blamed him for nearly everything - even the weather!'

Gemma smiled lovingly at her mother.

'I resented being in the house all day. I hated losing my freedom – two children meant that was it. I was a housewife, a mother, a nothing! Don't misunderstand me. I loved being your Mamma, but I lost my identity. I felt trapped! Though times are different, and young women have so much independence today, the emotions never change; you have to handle them along with everything else.'

'So how did you get through it? I've never felt this depressed and lonely before.'

'I know *bella*. I wished I could click my fingers and get you back to that happy place where you normally are... for me it was having a sermon from your papa's mamma.'

Gemma's eyes lit up on the mention of her Nan,

'What do you mean?' she asked.

'Well she had this way about her. As you know, at first we didn't see eye to eye. I had taken her little boy away from her. It was only four stops on the bus! But nevertheless she made it hard for me. so when she decided to give me some of her Celtic wisdom I resented it and told her where to stick her advice.'

'So how did that help?'

'It didn't,' she laughed. 'At first I was fuming! And again your poor papa took the brunt of it. It was around this time we moved out of the city, only an hour away from our families, but it felt like the other side of the world at the time. I was having a typical, miserable day when a song came on the radio that reminded me of our conversation. The more I turned the words over in my head the more it sounded like your grandmother. but without that annoying Irish accent that I could barely understand.'

'And your Italian accent wasn't annoying for her?'

'Of course not. My accent is beautiful!' Her mother smiled and gently laid Holly down under her activity gym. 'Well anyway, I started to realise that the family was my responsibility. Your papa was hard working and brought home all of the money at the time, so it was down to me to manage practically everything else. If I faltered then we would all fail and I couldn't live with that. Responsibility can be a burden, but is also a great gift.'

Without taking a breath she added, 'That was my calling at that time. I had to get on with life and do the best I could. As we say in Italia: *Siccome la casa brucia, riscaldiamoci*! Roughly that means: since the house is on fire let us warm ourselves! I chose to accept my gift, and well... '

'Did it all fall into place over night?'

'No darling, you were three, Jayne was six months old and every day was a struggle. But gradually

Jayne started sleeping through the night and I made some new friends down at the church. There was a mothers' group and it was great to mix with people in the same boat. Gradually things got a little more bearable. And every day I took time to appreciate my gift. Love, *bella*, love is the greatest gift.'

'Did you tell Nan she had helped?'

'No I wouldn't give her the satisfaction!' Her mother gave Gemma a hug and smiled at her, 'Am I going to get a coffee today or do I have to make it?'

'No Mamma, I can do that. One thing, what was the song?'

'Oh, an old Beatles thing. *Let it be*, I think it's called.'

Before leaving, her mother suggested she look after Holly a few days a week and then every other Saturday she could have all the kids, to give Gemma and Ryan some free time.

Keeping her promise, she was there on the dot every time; unflagging and full of energy. Her mother started to remind Gemma of her Nan when she had looked after her and Jayne in the school holidays but she thought twice about saying so.

After a couple of weeks of their new routine Gemma's mother encouraged her to start bringing Holly around to her house and then to go out for a while by herself if she felt up to it. She even gave her £200 to buy some new clothes for Spring.

Whilst this seemed like a wonderful treat at first, as Gemma slogged around the High Street trying to find clothes that suited her mood, and with more difficulty her figure, a renewed depression fell upon her. How had she let everything go?

Gemma plonked herself down at a table outside a coffee shop and sat people watching. She looked up and down the Street and noticed with dismay the number of shops that had closed, particularly the estate agents. She knew that many saw estate agents as overpaid leeches but that was never why she was in the business. They were a vital service even if most had forgotten that as they chased ever-spiralling commissions.

Gemma's mind started to whirl. She took a pen from her bag and started to scribble.

- Service
- Families
- Society

As she doodled around the words on the paper, her latte came and went cold beside her. Even though she never took even a sip, she did find the whole experience therapeutic. So, when her mother suggested she went out again she jumped at the chance and made a point of taking the time to chat to people in shops and restaurants. It was good to interact. To make conversation without having to explain her feelings and actions.

With an unwavering instinct Gemma's mother had guided her daughter towards the path to recovery and didn't miss a beat when picking up Gemma's negative vibes. She didn't push hard to get her back to her old happy go lucky self and nor did she coddle her. She was aware of every aspect of Gemma's psyche, even when Gemma wasn't. This enabled her to choose her moments carefully and deliberately.

And so it was as they watched the latest *Dragon's Den* on Sky Plus.

'That Duncan must have been the scariest ice cream man in the world! No wonder he gave it up to be a millionaire! But that James Caan's not bad for his age is he?' Her mother teased.

'I'm not even going to answer and get drawn into your sordid little mind,' Gemma replied.

'And as for that Peter Jones, he's too tall. I'd be nearly the same height as his...'

'Mamma, leave it!'

'An observation darling!' Then turning to Gemma her tone changed. 'There is something I've wanted to tell you for the past three months.'

Gemma looked a little apprehensive.

'You know your sister could never keep a secret? Well she still can't. She told me all about your new business back in December, more by accident really.'

'What? How could she? I didn't tell her!' Gemma squealed.

'Ryan did, I believe. After Holly was born. I think he was so scared about losing you and it slipped out. How hard you had been working and so on. It seems you thought we'd only be negative, and though I was a little upset it got me thinking. Since losing your papa maybe I have been too negative, but you can hardly blame me, waking up without his arms around me every day is heartbreaking. '

'I didn't mean it in a horrible way. I was worried you, or Jayne, would talk me out of it. Mamma, I'm sorry. '

'I know, *bella*. You were probably right, at the time, but now I feel more positive. Maybe it's having the grandchildren around me more or having a new baby in the family. It makes me realise how precious life is.'

'Mamma, what are you talking about? You have always appreciated life that's what so great about you. So what do you think of the idea?'

'This may surprise you, but I think it's excellent, I would have loved the opportunity to have tried it myself. If you present it well it could benefit a lot of people. I think you might be on to something special.'

'I didn't expect you to say that.' Gemma gasped.

'It's no good getting older without getting wiser,' she laughed, then hearing Holly stirring in her cot upstairs she jumped up, 'I'll get her. I want to get something else too.'

Within a few minutes she was back in the front room with Holly cradled in one arm and a book with an envelope sticking out of it in her other hand. Comforting Holly she handed the book to Gemma, 'This was one of your papa's books, I must have read it 10 times this past year and wanted you to read it too.'

She read the cover out loud, *Feel The Fear And Do It Anyway* by Susan Jeffers. Thanks, I have heard of it.'

'Yes she is very well known. She's an amazing lady with great ideas, like you, *bella*.'

'I don't know about that,' Gemma responded coyly, flicking through the dog-eared book she noticed several mentions of the Law of Attraction which sparked greater interest. As Gemma eagerly thumbed through the pages she stopped at the envelope.

'Only open it when I have said my piece', her mother said, 'I love your idea so much that I would love to invest in it, all done properly of course, like a business angel, not like that hard faced Deborah woman off the TV though; I'm far sexier.'

'I don't know what to say.'

'Try thank you,' her mother joked.

'Very funny, I mean there is no business yet, just an idea.'

'Well I hope you don't mind but Ryan gave me Hilary's number, and though I've always thought she was a stuck up cow, it's turned out she is really lovely and hasn't stopped moving forward with your plans. She's waiting for you to dot the Is and cross the Ts.'

Gemma sat dumbstruck, looking at her mother as she played with Holly's hair.

'I don't believe it,' she finally said.

'Well you better had, Ryan has registered the domain name and set up a company at Companies House. All it needs is for you to be ready to put it in your name. How do you like the sound of Estate Angels Direct?'

Opening the envelope Gemma saw a cheque for £4,000.

'It was from your papa's life insurance *bella*, and I know he would have believed in your idea too.'

'Wow, thanks Mamma, I'm really speechless, I have to have a little time to think.'

'Of course, but we all believe in you. We love you. The big question is, are you ready to believe in yourself?'

On the drive home Gemma, instead of feeling elated, was fuming about the little conspiracy going on behind her back.

'Have I really been that hard to communicate with? How dare they think they know what's right for me.'

Eventually she pulled onto the drive and scooping up Holly, rushed indoors. Ryan was at the kitchen table helping the kids with their homework. Gemma gently passed the baby to Katie, looked at Ryan and then, throwing her arms around him, burst into tears.

## 7: Fake It Till You Make It!

# Life SPARKL<u>E</u>S

*Enthusiasm is contagious. Be a carrier.*
Susan Rabin

Hilary had been discussing how far she had moved forward with the business for under an hour. Gemma was totally captivated by Hilary's eagerness and zest but despite the recent attentions of those around her, or perhaps because of them, Gemma still felt unable to really add much to the conversation herself. She nodded and made the right noises to keep Hilary flowing.

The content of their first real chat for over three months had startled Gemma. There was so much going on. The most significant development was that the first couple Hilary had signed up had become champion associates already. Their names were Moses and Khadijah and, together with their eldest son Jude, were proposing to start a pilot scheme over the next three weeks! Hilary assured Gemma of their professionalism and couldn't wait for her to meet them.

'They have not taken over, I assure you, but they are extremely enthusiastic and cannot wait to get started. They have been amazing at putting me in touch with the local network and, if it is okay with you, sweetie, we have provisionally booked a function room at the Beau Regard Hotel to do a presentation to select agents next month.'

Gemma had mixed feelings.

She felt like an outsider on her own project. And, with the words her mother had spoken the previous week about the need for self belief ringing through her ears, it was not an exaggeration to state Gemma felt a little dizzy.

In her heart there was little doubt the concept would work. It now appeared to have also caught the imaginations of others. So much so, in truth, it could work with or without her input. Most people had no idea who she was anyway. Perhaps, Gemma reasoned, it should remain that way.

After the meeting Gemma returned to her mother's to pick up Holly.

'How did it all go?' her mother asked as Gemma fussed around the sofa gathering Holly's things.

'Oh, appears there's a lot happening. The pilot scheme will be starting in three weeks with a couple of seminars in town. Might be good.'

'You don't sound very enthusiastic. I hope you aren't presenting the seminar – you'll have to get Hilary pole-dancing in the background to keep them interested!'

Gemma was taken a little by surprise by her mother's comments. Granted she was known for her sharp wit and sometimes caustic tongue but it hadn't ever been aimed at Gemma before. After all this was where she came for comfort and a kind word. Gemma remained silent and looked sheepish.

'*Bella* darling,' her mother started, 'you have been through so much these past three months. My heart bled dry to see you so physically and mentally drained. But look at you! You made it! Little by little, day by day.' She smiled lovingly at her daughter, 'I guess that when Winston Churchill said *"When going through hell keep going"* he wasn't talking about Great Britain facing up to its greatest nightmare ever. No, it was purely aimed at poor old Clementine giving birth!'

Gemma finally relented. 'Now you do sound like Nan going on about the war.'

'You're not too old to put over my knee, *bella* ' she said jokingly, 'but I will add one more thing, that I must admit comes from your grandmother. The reason birds fly is that they take themselves lightly.'

'Yes Mamma, I know exactly what you mean, and I am trying.'

'I know you are, darling. I am so proud of both of my girls. But we all only have so much time. No more. Like that young girl, what is her name? Jade Goody. And your friend, Pauline. Before you know it our time will come to pass. And when we are on our deathbeds it will be the things we didn't do that haunt us - not the things we did.'

Her mother made a cross in front of her body with her right hand and closed her eyes. When she re-opened them a huge smile spread across her face lighting up the room.

'I won't go on. But please remember *bella*, *If only* are the two saddest words in the English language.'

True to her word Gemma's mother did not mention anything about business for the rest of the afternoon; it was only on leaving that she thrust a piece of paper into Gemma's hand. The note bore the addresses of two internet networking websites.

On returning home Gemma was greeted by Ryan at the door. He gave her a swift peck on the lips, brought Holly in from the car, and then returned to the kitchen to help Sam finish his homework. It sounded as though Katie had finished hers already as Abba came booming out of the front room. Popping her head around the door Gemma saw her 10-year old dancing and singing her heart out to *Mamma Mia*.

Before Gemma could disappear back into the kitchen she was spotted.

'Mum, Mum, come and dance with me,' pleaded Katie.

'No not now, honey, I'm tired.'

'Please Mum. We haven't danced for years!'

'That's a bit of an exaggeration, cheeky.'

'Maybe,' Katie said with a smile. 'Come on please... My favourite song's on next.'

'Okay, Okay.'

Katie enthusiastically grabbed her Mum's hand and led the way as the sound of *Money, Money, Money* echoed in their ears.

Katie then fast forwarded the DVD to the next song and Gemma collapsed onto the sofa, exhausted but laughing. Katie threw herself next to her Mum and snuggled into her for a super-sized hug,

'See, you can still do it, Mum.'

'Maybe,' Gemma replied still gasping for air, 'I need a little more time and practice.'

In a fit of the giggles Katie spluttered, 'There's always time to dance, Silly! You don't need to practice – do it! Unless you're too old?'

'You really are getting too cheeky little lady,' and with that Gemma tickled Katie until eventually she submitted.

'Now, repeat after me. Mummy isn't too old'

'Okay Mummy's not tooo old! She's just... well padded!'

'Why Katie, you little moo! That does it. Let's see how well padded you are!'

And the tickling game went into overdrive as Katie squealed with delight.

Finally they settled down and cuddled; watching the remainder of the film. Totally unaware of the impact her words had had on her mother, Katie sat mesmerised by the music. Gemma sat mesmerised by her beautiful daughter.

*Always remember to forget*
*The troubles that passed away,*
*But never forget to remember*
*The blessings that came each day.*
(Yet another traditional Irish saying)

Before Gemma knew it, the weekend was back. Her mother had already been to pick up the kids and she was having an extra lie in. She sipped her morning cup of tea Ryan had brought up to her and quietly thought about the past few months.

Gemma was relieved to find that her days were more recognisable now, and no longer resembled Ground Hog Day. Each day had definition and became more than a constant stream of feeding, nappies, feeding, and more nappies.

She was grateful her family had got on with life after the birth of Holly. More thanks to Ryan, and her mother, than her but there's no use dwelling on the negative This was no time for regrets. She could sense some light at the end of the tunnel.

Katie's youthful wisdom had certainly refreshed the parts other beers cannot reach!

Where did that come from? A sure sign of too much telly quoting vintage advertisements when pondering the meaning of life, Gemma thought.

But it was also a sure sign of recovery. Maybe it was because spring was in the air but recently she felt more at peace within her own body and mind. Her conversation with her eldest daughter reminded Gemma of a quote she had heard, 'Life is not a dress rehearsal', by Rose Tremain. Katie said it much better, Gemma decided: You don't need to practise – do it!

She put her tea down and reached into her bedside cabinet pulling out her pen and Golden Notebook. She had briefly looked at it the previous week and was impressed with the enthusiastic tone of her writing. She had found her own words as motivating and inspiring as any self help book she had read. And yet, she hadn't listened to her old thoughts in her darkest hours. Instead Gemma knew she had chosen to be dictated by the minute-to-minute needs of a life that seemed to be spiralling out of control! Had it not been for the love and support of those close to her maybe it would have.

So maybe some things do benefit from regular practice, she wondered. Good habits, developing a new skill? Building a positive routine and maintaining it even when the you-know-what hits the thingamajig!

With the notebook opened to her last entry Gemma wrote...

> Use it or lose it!!

Then she noticed that she hadn't completed anything under the headings of Love or Enthusiasm. Her SPARKLE acronym was incomplete.

Gemma hesitated. This was the first time she had even contemplated trying to write out her feelings for over three months. It felt awkward, but she persevered.

> It's exactly when I am feeling bad that I need to work at feeling good.
>
> I knew I had the framework to move on with life but I ignored it and tucked it away out of sight, hoping to get back to it when the fog had lifted. But it never lifted because that was all I could see and all I concentrated on.
>
> Like attracts like! Always!
>
> Moving directly from misery to bliss is impossible but by being a little bit better in that moment from the last I will get there! I GOT THERE!

> In future I will build and maintain a healthy routine to keep focused.
>
> But don't forget to let go as well. Enjoy the journey – every step!
>
> And DANCE!!

Gemma had a sip of her tea and tried to dispel the self talk that she could have overcome her own despair by focusing on the positive sides of life even earlier. 'Everything has it's time,' she murmured. 'What's done is done. I can't change the past. Learn and move on!'

She then returned to her SPARKLE acronym.

## Love

> Before truly loving someone else you must learn to love and accept yourself first. Even liking yourself is a start.

Hold on, LOVE is at the root of everything but it's not what the L stands for!

Gemma had had a pure, blinding eureka moment.

> L is for Learning!

## Learning

> - Never stop learning.
> - Valuable lessons can come from the most unlikely teachers – Mum, Nan, KATIE, even myself!
> - Read widely and wisely
> - Education, Education, Education!
> - When you have nothing left to learn – you die!

Gemma smiled to herself and then quickly made several comments on Enthusiasm, her brain had already started to quicken its response and she could slightly sense the flow returning.

## Enthusiasm

- Constantly surround myself with positive images to boost my motivation, create my own little space – a noticeboard where I can pin pictures from magazines of things I desire.
- Keep enthusiastic people close to me as I'm sure it rubs off.
- Keep toxic people away for the same reason.
- Share my feelings more with Ryan again so that when I get down he can push these pages in front of me as a reminder of who I truly am.
- Try and take an hour a day to sharpen my own saw without feeling guilty.
- SMILE.
- And share the gift of enthusiasm with others – like love there's more than enough to go around!
- Enthusiasm is energy in human form (Hey, that's good!)
- And on the days I don't feel it... then...

Suddenly she heard Ryan running back up the stairs, 'Only meee!'

'Really, I was expecting Vinnie Jones.'

'Very funny,' he laughed as he dropped his dressing gown to the floor, 'before you spoil the moment, any chance of a cuddle?'

'Let me write one more thing and I'm all yours,' she grinned:

If all else fails... FAKE IT!

# 8: Don't Look Back in Anger

# Life SPARKLE<u>S</u>

*Many things in life will catch your eye,
but very few will catch your heart.*

'I don't believe it! What a bloody parasite.'

'What's wrong?'

'I'm speechless; you take a look yourself, babe.'

Ryan slid the paper across the glass patio table as Gemma eased herself from her reclined sun lounger. Squinting in the early morning sun she read the headline and the first few paragraphs out loud.

> Another dragon! Entrepreneur of the year Gemma Lewis may have warmed our hearts with her apparent rise to success but in her wake she has left a trail of broken hearts. Hard-faced business woman Gemma sacrificed life with her devoted husband for the bright lights of success. Rob Catley, 42, has revealed for the first time how he guided Gemma on her road to fame and fortune and then was dumped out of the blue at the first taste of success, leaving him homeless, distraught and with his own business in tatters.

'Tosser!' Gemma spluttered as she threw the paper back to Ryan.

'Charming! Don't shoot the messenger!'

'Very funny,' she chuckled as her anger subsided a little, 'I can't believe he would stoop that low. '

'It could be worse; it could have been on the front page instead of being tucked away on page seven. Anyhow it's all lies – who's going to believe him or believe that you are a hard-nosed bitch – I can vouch that you cry watching Bambi.'

'Yeah, I guess so.' she said reluctantly. 'You cried too!' she added.

'Exactly, you would have to be dead hard not to.'

'A blancmange is harder than you!'

'Oi, don't push it, I'm all man you know.'

'Oh, I know. 'Gemma leaned over for a quick kiss.

In her heart she knew Ryan was right, there wasn't too much to get stressed over. She was renting a luxurious villa in Sardinia for the whole of the summer holidays. Mixing a couple of hours of work in the morning with a few Skype calls, e-mails and writing, then heading off for lunch in town. Other important appointments included the beach, lazing by the pool or watching the kids play. The evenings were often spent watching the sun set with a nice bottle of Rioja, just her and Ryan.

Dreams do come true she thought, especially if you are persistent, can handle a little rejection and know the direction you want to take. There is always a way to improve your circumstances.

Her thoughts returned to Rob and imagined the sheepish look he would give the next time he bothered to take the kids out, and how pathetic his life had become; caught up in the past, holding grudges that were filled with slow corrosive anger.

Maybe the opinions of a sad and bitter ex-husband, out to make some quick cash, should not really concern her. After the initial shock of seeing her name in the paper she felt more pity for him than anger. What was the point of being angry; he had no control over her feelings any more.

She vividly recalled the time he came to collect Sam for a football match. It was shortly after Holly's birth and Gemma was still struggling to hold it together. She opened the door to see Rob attached to an over keen 20-something with more piercings than original thoughts and was greeted with 'Gems, you look rough! Have you met Kandi? She's an art student.'

'No, I haven't had the pleasure. So, Kandi, what medium do you prefer, fingerpaint or Play-Doh?'

Ouch!

The Coven relished the retelling of that story. Toni was a particular fan.

'It's about time you grew some balls!' she'd say. Maybe I am hardening up, Gemma thought ... but to resort to telling lies about me?

Anyhow, fortunately, she had an interview set up tomorrow with the prominent *Business Life* magazine; the journalist and photographer were flying in for the day, to feature her as a Mummy Magnate. If they broached the subject of her ex then she would answer as truthfully and tactfully as possible and quickly move on to more important topics.

Since winning the prestigious Entrepreneur of the Year Award her life had become a whirlwind. From the presentation by Sir Richard Branson through countless interview requests; offers of joint ventures to renewing old friendships from school, via her newly updated Facebook page – Gemma was slightly giddy with all the success. It was exhausting but she also had an amazing sense of satisfaction.

In her heart, as much as the recognition and success of her networking business made her feel great, she still remained grounded. Recognising that whilst the limelight was on her it was the business idea that was the real success story. Soon the crowds would be moving on to the next flavour of the month. The best she could hope for would be that her legacy would empower and inspire others to have a go!

For now though she would milk it for all it was worth. If only the world could see her trying to get the kids to school on time, cleaning up the family mess and ironing enough clothes for a small battalion in her fluffy white slipper boots and tea stained dressing gown. The wonders of PR!

The pretty journalist settled into a comfy chair and laid out her A4 pad, pen and recorder on the glass table. With the parasol up, and a jug of iced fresh orange overflowing with fruit ready to pour, the interview was set to go.

After the initial formalities the journalist guided the conversation in a friendly, professional manner. Gemma was impressed by the young woman's attitude. Though feeling relaxed she didn't want to end up being caught off guard. As polite as the woman opposite appeared Gemma knew she wouldn't hesitate to go for the jugular if she saw a sign of weakness.

No, not all publicity is good publicity. A bad interview now, especially after the kiss and tell porkies job by Rob, could ruin her business. And where would that leave her faithful group of networkers who had helped her build the company? This was not her baby now – this was her family.

'Stay focused, stay focused,' she repeated to herself.

Journalist: *I absolutely love what you have achieved over the past few years and have followed your company with an avid interest. It looks like a really exciting and interesting way to work. You must be very proud. Do you want to tell us a little bit about the company first? That's probably a good place to start.*

Gemma: *Thanks. It is a fun environment in our small Head Office; we try our best to be innovative, and we keep in touch with our home business network and registered property agents at least once a week.*

> *As you are aware we are still focused on the property sector as our core business. And we've created a niche market by giving vendors choice across many estate agent outlets.*
>
> *The traditional estate agent still receives their share of the pie, albeit slightly less, but it frees up their time to focus on those vendors who require extra help. Yet the best bit is they still earn a passive income that they may otherwise have lost. And that's where our network of home business agents comes into it. They help vendors with details of their homes and chain progress etc.*

Journalist: *You sure make it sound simple.*

Gemma: *Exactly! By keeping things as simple as possible everyone understands the system and this reduces conflict and duplication of effort..*

Journalist: *With a system so simple aren't you afraid someone will come along and steal your idea and over take your position?*

Gemma: *No of course not. If others can maintain the same level of passion as us and compete with our spirit of customer focus then they deserve the position. More competition can only make us more creative and innovative.*

Journalist: *You are so passionate about what you do, what do you put that down to?*

Gemma: *I always say it's the way my mother put my hat on. My mum always says a life without passion isn't a life. Unfortunately for some, I know no other way to be!*

Journalist: *I'll have to remember that one in the future; it was my mother who made me such an inquisitive person, perfect for a journalist.*

Gemma: *Yes I guess it does help to be nosy!*

Journalist: *I walked straight into that one, didn't I?*

They both burst out laughing. And Gemma felt at ease, but she still reminded herself to stay focused.

Journalist: *We all owe a lot to our mothers in many ways.*

Gemma: *Yes we do. We all should appreciate them a little more I guess. During our time as parents we all wear many hats; teacher, emotional and physical caregiver, peacemaker, negotiator and role model amongst many others. We all have this natural ability as parents to be instinctive; sometimes we need a little more self-confidence to channel it into other areas of our lives.*

*And though the majority of our networkers are mothers I must add that we do not only recruit women and we are in no way ultra feminist in our attitudes, it so happens the hours and skill set required appeals more to women than men.*

Journalist: *I know what you mean. I get a strong impression that the most successful women in business today are finding alternatives to traditional working practices rather than trying to fit into old moulds. But these new family-friendly companies can be attractive to men as well; after all our views around balancing work and family life are changing.*

Gemma: *Exactly!*

*That's why winning the Entrepreneur of the Year award was so special. Of course I am as proud of my earlier Mumpreneur Award as well, but, society is forever trying to pigeon hole us in some way and narrow our options. I am a Mum and an entrepreneur - my business is as good as any other. I am proud of all my achievements. None of us have to be what others want us to be; we're all free to be what we want to be. It's all about self-belief. Be yourself, believe in yourself and do what works best for you.*

Journalist: *Wow! There's that passion overflowing again.*

Gemma: *Yeah, I told you. I can't help it! But I can't overemphasise that passion is the foundation of any business or personal relationship. Being passionate informs your decisions, and your decisions help you take action. And your actions decide your life. On the other side of the coin passion with no action leaves you with dreams. Action turns dreams into reality.*

Journalist: *Very true.*

*I believe you started your business when you were pregnant with child number three, is that right?*

Gemma: *Yes I did. It was so hard to define at the time but I had never felt more enthusiastic and creative in my life. In hindsight when I was pregnant with Sam I was feeling artistic but never really followed it through. But with Holly I went with the flow. I felt compassion for the estate agents who were losing their jobs and saw a solution for some of them. I looked around and asked lots of questions and created my formula. Once I had the map I suppose I morphed into Lara Croft – nothing was insurmountable. I thought if it's not out there, I'm going to find ways of creating it myself, and if and when I do, I'm going to share it with others. It was a rocky road but gradually I started to have the faith in myself that others already had and, now I want to create that faith in others.*

Journalist: *Well there are a lot of people out there now who are grateful you did.*

*With everything you do, including bringing up three children, you must be shattered by the end of the day?*

Gemma: *Yes I am, but I am no super-mum, honestly. There's a whole team behind me and the relationships we have built in the company are our greatest asset. Sounds like a cliché, I know, but it's true. Our people really are the glue that has held us together through thick and thin.*

Journalist: *Great stuff. Do you always get it right first time when it comes to relationships?*

Here we go,' Gemma thought, 'I was beginning to like this woman and now she wants to dish the dirt! Don't bite, Gems.'

Gemma: *No, not at all. Unfortunately, we all make mistakes. But the key is to learn from them and not repeat them. Sometimes it feels more like a learning mountain than a learning curve! Ultimately we must have trust between each other and in ourselves. Building that trust is an important part of our business ethos.*

*You have hit upon my favourite subject, and what I believe is the major failure in both relationships and business as a whole. Would you like me to share it with you? As I can go off on a tangent given the chance. I think it's the Gemini in me!*

Journalist: *Of course. Please do. You can't leave me hanging now!*

Gemma: *Okay. It's quite simple really. In life we all live on four separate plains - our Emotional, Mental, Spiritual and Physical worlds.*

*The first three are reflected in our physical world.*

*The trouble is that the society we live in today tends to focus too much on the physical world and materialistic accumulation.*

*We end up neglecting the most critical aspects of our being. We are mistrustful of others and, worse still, of our own wisdom which stems from the other plains. And it's this listening and willingness to learn from your deepest feelings and gut instinct that can lead to a total transformation in your relationships, beliefs and attitude in life.*

Journalist: *Of course we have all heard of the saying mind, body and spirit before. But what has this to do with building a business?*

Gemma: *I know it sounds a little foreign at first. And I used to think this kind of talk*

> *was mumbo jumbo and not for the real world. But the more I've allowed myself to be guided by my inner voice, the better my intuition and life has become. Though of course not everything is perfect all the time, but my attitude sees me through the darker days a lot more easily than it used to – I'm a firm believer that tomorrow will be a brighter day.*
>
> *I guess it's more about going with the flow of life instead of battling against it; and knowing yourself a little better.*

Journalist: *That's a brilliant philosophy and not mumbo jumbo at all. I've heard a lot worse, believe me!*

They both laughed and reached for their drinks at the same time.

Journalist: *So what, in your opinion, is the definition of knowing?*

Gemma took another long sip of her orange and gazed down from her hillside retreat over the brush of pine trees and out to the glistening Mediterranean Sea. She came to focus on a lone fishing boat bobbing gently in the late morning sunshine, a few hundred metres from the coast, and a wry smile crossed her lips.

The journalist followed her gaze.

Journalist: *That looks like the life, doesn't it? I bet that fisherman doesn't have a care in the world.*

Gemma: *Yes, it does look quite relaxing. And that fisherman is probably a great example of knowing.*

Journalist: *How do you mean?*

Gemma: *Well, his family have most likely fished in these waters for generations. He probably learnt his trade from his father. But today our fisherman is probably kitted out with some modern state-of-the-art sonar device that can pick up shoals of fish. All he has to do is learn how to use it, plug it in and go. Much quicker, and certainly more efficient... when it works. But what happens on the days his device is not charged or becomes faulty? Can he rely on his innate ability to detect his catch, much like his grandfather and father would have done decades before? If he panics he will fail, but if he allows himself to* feel *his way back, he will find the fish. They are still there. He has to listen to his gut. We are all constantly learning new things, and technology and advances in knowledge can really help us be more effective, but it is important to remember that there are things we just* know *– the answers, like the fish are always there.*

Journalist: *Wow! I'd never have thought of it like that before.*

Gemma: *Me neither, the boat just caught my eye. Maybe that's what I mean about being open to your own inner voice and creativity. But it's also about trust as I said before but this time trusting yourself.*

Journalist: *Very true. So in essence it's a fact and feeling pick and mix. There's plenty of choice and new flavours are bring added all the time. You can take the advice of others and try different combinations,*

|  | *there is no one way. In the end you know what works best for you.* |
|---|---|
| Gemma: | *I couldn't have put it better!* |
|  | *Taking my fisherman idea one step further I guess we could easily say we all have an inbuilt sonar device in our brains, which can be used to detect opportunities, forewarn us of danger and guide us when we have doubt. The trouble with many people is that they don't switch theirs on.* |
| Journalist: | *Which I guess leads people to stick in their ruts and not follow through on their ideas?* |
| Gemma: | *Yes I guess it is, and at the end of the day you can only help and encourage those who want to improve their own environment, however much as you may wish to help or see a better way ahead for them.* |
| Journalist: | *Before I leave you and your family in peace to enjoy the rest of your day I want to thank you for taking the time to talk to me. It has been totally different from the usual mundane interviews I do about balance sheets, stock prices and talk of recession. Your enthusiasm and zest for life are truly inspiring.* |
| Gemma: | *Thank you, you're always welcome.* |
| Journalist: | *Finally, I have one more question that I would like to ask you. You have been quoted as saying your mother was a great influence in your life. What has been the best advice she has passed onto you?* |

Gemma paused and then carefully answered.

Gemma: *Yes, she has been a tower of strength on more than one occasion. But I have been really lucky to be positively influenced by not only my Mother but also by both my Grandmothers and Father as well. I can't say Mum passed on one piece of advice I could share - it was more the example Mamma set for us. She always worked hard and with great passion and unconditional love.*

*My father on the other hand would often say something to me when I was a teenager, although it took me a while to realise exactly what he meant. And that was:*

## *Many things in life will catch your eye, but only a few will catch your heart.*

Journalist: *That is beautiful. What do you think he meant?*

Gemma: *Don't do what others want you to do or chase other people's dreams. Look, do you know what started all this? Finding a card my Nan sent me on my 18th birthday. I have it here.*

*Gemma passed the old card to the journalist and waited as she read.*

Journalist: *Remember always to trust your own heart. Everything will be fine. Just SPARKLE!*

*That's sweet... And Sparkle? That's a great little word isn't it?*

Gemma: *It certainly is.*

| | |
|---|---|
| Journalist: | *Thanks for sharing your deepest thoughts. You have so much wisdom to share. Maybe you should write a book?* |
| | *Gemma's almond green eyes sparkled and a soft knowing smile lit up her face.* |
| Gemma: | *Now there's an idea!* |

Susan Ödev & Mark Weeks

# Part Three

# Meet The Mum Ultrapreneurs

Over the summer of 2009 I (Susan) interviewed over 30 business mums from all across the UK and Ireland. Most of these were successfully recorded and will be made available as audio files free on our website *www.mum-ultrapreneur.com/bonuses*. Please take the time to pop over to the site and listen to these amazing women talk about their businesses and their motivation to become Mum Ultrapreneurs.

The following pages contain extracts from these conversations following the acronym

### SPARKLES

Read them through in one hit or dip in and out whenever you need inspiration. Some of these business mums have been growing their families and their businesses together for up to 20 years. Others are just starting out. Full details of their businesses can also be found on our website by following their links.

Here come the girls. Enjoy!

# S is for Simplicity

As Gemma declutters her life, her mind declutters too and her ideas become clearer. There is an expression: Keep It Simple Stupid and looking around it seems that the best business ideas are the simplest. Don't expect to do it all. Clear away the unnecessary, clarify your goals and priorities and focus on how to make things as simple as possible. And do not dismiss an idea for being too simple – there is no such thing in business. Consider the concept of bottled water or eBay or Cabbage Patch Dolls! All very simple, but extremely successful, ideas.

When we take the product to a baby show, people always say *I can't believe I didn't think of this because it's so simple. Cuddledry* is an example of simplicity in terms of context and design, and shows you do not have to have a brilliant scientific brain to come up with a marketable idea. And by the same token, you don't necessarily have to have lots and lots of money to spend on developing a product. Some things you can do very, very simply. You can start very small and then grow as and when it suits you and your lifestyle.

Helen Wooldridge, Cuddledry,
*www.cuddledry.com,* Somerset, England

I developed *Mummy Must Have* after the birth of my second child. He had developed colic at three weeks and it was extremely distressing for all of the family really. I had a two-year-old at home and at the time was finding it very difficult to try and calm an upset screaming baby. Whatever I was finding out there available to me, it wasn't meeting the needs of my baby and, you know, the distress was getting worse and worse. I learned that swaddling nice and tightly was important to help comfort them. But my baby would kick off every product on the market so I decided to develop my own swaddling product that couldn't be kicked off.

Monic Joint, Mummy Must Have,
*www.mummymusthave.com*, Southampton, England

Susan, for me, the word *simple* is completely behind our whole model and the way we approached this project. Like you say, the product is simple, my supply chain is simple. I'm very, very clear on my capacity of how much time and energy I can devote to driving the business forward. Don't over complicate things. You don't need to start with a perfect business.

Rita Derkatsch Nagy, Ming-Cha Tea,
*www.ming-cha.co.uk*, London, England

I wanted something that was a simple idea and that was really simple to operate, because starting up on your own can be quite scary so it was very important to get something manageable. The simplicity thing comes into the design format of the website. I wanted to keep it very specialised and very easy to use. I kept it very clear. People keep coming to the site because they know they can find what they are looking for very quickly.

If it's a simple idea but it already exists, there's nothing to actually stop you doing it and doing it better. Putting your little spin, your angle on it, and the fact that it is an idea that's out there already, normally is an idea that works, so it is still worth pursuing.

Joanna Pearce, Nappy Valley, *www.nappyvalley.co.uk*, London and Guildford, England

I love being around people. I'd done a lot of travelling and I wanted to think about how I could share my experiences. To go into the travel industry and have my own shop as a travel agency seemed a simple way to go. I could offer people a personal service and give them this independent, unbiased knowledge that you probably can't get from searching on an internet search engine. Yes, it was a simple idea to set the business up and as in anything, stay focused and follow it through with your vision. Keep your eye on your goal and be patient.

Karen Simmonds, Travel Matters, *www.travelmatters.co.uk*, London, England

The idea of running a music group really is a very simple idea and because of that in some respects it was very easy to develop. We did have more complex issues when it became more than a hobby and I think people need to keep that in mind. Things like music clearance and establishing a company and registering a trademark, but all of those evolved from a very simple idea.

Karen Sherr, Musical Minis,
*www.musicalminis.co.uk*, Middlesex, England

OK, so 10 years ago I had the baby and was looking for products for his really bad skin problems. This led me to look into the whole baby products market and the things they were putting on the skin. I got quite frightened by all the ingredients, and so decided to start a business around that to sell natural products for babies.

The first product was washable nappies because I found that the chemicals they were using in the disposables were quite scary. I based the whole business around that. I thought it'd be quite fun to have a little shop, and my son would come into the shop with me and we'd hang out there but then I realised within a few weeks that I was on to something good.

It's a simple idea but you must have the drive to push it through to that next stage. If it was all simple, then we'd all be doing it, wouldn't we?

Jill Barker, Green Baby,
*www.greenbaby.co.uk*, London, England

I would give this piece of advice to any small business out there. if you're targeting other small or even big businesses, remember people are busy and they don't have the time to do everything for themselves. So, for example, if I am sitting here and I hate my PC, it's always crashing, but I got an e-mail in my inbox that said 'Are you a small business and haven't got a clue how to work your PC, do you need some help? I'm a chappie who can help you,' I'd think, Thank goodness, someone has come to save the day. And honestly, the people I targeted, they were all in the same position. They knew that they needed to be getting their brands out there, but they didn't know where to start... And so by me sending them a note, it takes that hassle away from them. It's a win win, and it's a very simple idea. And it's worked consistently for me.

Melissa Talago, PeekaBoo Communications,
www.peekaboocoms.co.uk, Berkshire, England

I thought no, it's too simple an idea, (I actually had the idea in Vietnam. My mum and dad were with us when we adopted the baby.). So I thought Could we do it? And Are there other people doing it? We looked around and we found out that actually, no, people were bringing in the knock off type of handbag, from the Far East, you know, the Guess or the Prada. But they (didn't) seem to be bringing in these absolutely beautiful bags. I grew up with Avon ladies coming around, with my mum holding Tupperware parties and china parties and dress parties. It seemed a very easy way to go and because it was new and because no one had seen these kinds of bags before, you could guarantee to get people to turn up.

Anne Ryan, Handbag Heaven,
*www.handbagheaven.ie*, Dublin, Ireland

It came down to the fact that it was something that I wanted to use and it didn't exist. There wasn't anywhere you could send something beautifully packaged for less than £10, a little something that fits through a letterbox.. I've worked in the e-commerce industry for the last five years managing different websites and the most common customer complaint was not being able to be in to sign for the parcel. So really it was the very simple idea of making something bespoke that can fit through a letterbox and the concept grew from there. How can we make it easy for someone to purchase and then also for the recipient to receive? It's as simple as that.

Claire Wilson, Send A Thought,
*www.sendathought.co.uk*, London, England

Right at the beginning, people said you can't do big bras. You need to do all cup sizes and we said no, we want to focus on big cup sizes. It's going to be special because its big cup sizes and we've absolutely stuck to that. And it is quite a simple concept. We think, does it work within the context of Bravissimo and I think it is clearer if it's simpler. Obviously then you can go into other areas. We started with big bras and now we've done swimwear, nightwear and clothing but it's still focused on the same customer.

Sarah Tremellen, Bravissimo,
*www.bravissimo.com*, Leamington Spa, England

My simple idea was to offer free advice and support for mums online. That's the basic idea and simple is best when it comes to businesses.

Scot Mum is an online community for mums in Scotland fundamentally it's for mums by mums and that's the whole essence of the web site.

Hannah Young, Scot Mum,
*www.scotmum.com*, Edinburgh, Scotland

I think it's the simplest ideas that work. And mine is to keep everything as natural as possible... It's really quite an intimate/sensitive time especially when you've just had a baby and you don't want to be in a studio in front of bright lights. You know, I really felt that there was a gap in the market for a woman to come out and use the natural environment. I want people to walk in and say, that's a beautiful photo. They don't care where it's taken. It's that stunning. And that was my simple idea. Keep it really, really natural.

Vicki Knights, Family Photographer,
*www.vickiknights.co.uk*, London, England

There were various motives I guess, Susan, with my business head on, the Work and Families Act 2006 was going to take effect from April 2007, meaning that women were potentially taking a longer break from the work place. Employers were going to start thinking about how to retain women and how to support them through that long absence from work.

There were government reports coming out from the Women and Work Commission, suggesting that the crucial time where women fall out of the workplace was around giving birth and the children starting school So there was a business imperative, but I can say, personally, the first year of being a mother of two was probably the hardest time I've been through in terms of being personally challenged to just get on with it, and feel that I was doing OK and being as I wanted to be. I thought, I've got all these coaching and consultancy training skills... I knew a lot about facilitating a room full of managers and skills for getting by myself but could I get my three-year old to get his shoes on at the right moment?

So I started organising parent coaching groups because I wanted to contribute something to people in that same position.

Jennifer Liston-Smith, Managing Maternity Ltd
*www.managingmaternity.co.uk*, Llanelwy, Wales

You don't have to go down the company route straight away. You can operate as a sole trader. Make sure you get your tax and insurance straight, and start from there.

With technology nowadays, you can give the impression that you are a multi person corporation when in reality you're somebody sitting at your kitchen table. My thought is certainly, starting off, keep it simple.

Darina Loakman, I am a WAHM,
*www.iamawahm.com*, Dublin, Ireland

I can't even begin to imagine not being with the kids during the day. I enjoy the time I'm spending with the kids. That makes it worthwhile. I can't imagine everything being set in a strict regime where I have to get really stressed in the morning, getting the kids ready before I go out to work, having to look good to go to work and put make up on and stuff. Even something as simple as that. You know, I sit at home in front of the computer when Robbie naps, in jeans and a jumper. I don't have to worry about what I look like. And, you know, that lessens the stress.

Victoria Dixon, Enhance Me,
*www.enhance-me.com*, Orkney, Scotland

> It was relatively easy for me to set up my business but in saying that, obviously, running a business is not simple when you're trying to run a home and look after your children as well... You know, I laugh at these people, they ring, and they say, 'Can you put me onto your accounts department? I am accounts and I am sales and I am everything. They think because it's an online business that it's in some office somewhere. They don't realise that it's like my fourth bedroom. I think, you know, you have to keep it relatively simple to keep your sanity.
>
> Tara McCormack, Cardmagical and Berry Wild Jam
> *www.cardmagical.com*, Co. Cavan, Ireland

> I don't know what it is, but we are inclined to over complicate things and I've been guilty of it Particularly us mums, because we're juggling a lot of balls, we're very reactive, and It's only when we actually sit down and think about what we're doing, do we really get to consider whether this is actually the simplest way to get from a to b.
>
> Natalie Lue, London, England,
> Self Employed Mum (*www.selfemployedmum.co.uk*),
> Baggage Reclaim (*www.baggagereclaim.co.uk*),
> Bambino Goodies (*www.bambinogoodies.co.uk*),
> Nest Goodies (*www.nestgoodies.co.uk*)

I think that's very significant Susan because I think that there is a belief system for a lot of mums that you can't have a child and have a life. The thing about being self employed, about following our own dreams is that it fits in perfectly with being a full time mother. I can write, you know, when my little one is asleep... I have my computer and my desk in my kitchen, so that I can do some admin, I can cook a meal, I can read a story book with her, I can come back to my computer again, I can pick things up and put things down. If I was in a full time job, I wouldn't be able to do this.

Martine Brennan, Contented Living Publishing and Coaching, *www.contentedliving.com* and Author of *Happiness It's Just A Habit*, *www.happinessitsjustahabit.com*, Co. Kerry, Ireland

I think your acronym really shows that it's sometimes about being brave. I was saying if it feels right, you have just got to do it. Actually it feels right, maybe after doing it. When we first talked about launching this, quite a few people were asking 'but why isn't anybody else doing it? Why does it not exist yet?' The businesses that often stand out are the ones that are brave and trying to do something different, although it feels risky at times.

Sophie Devonshire, Babes With Babies, *www.babeswithbabies.com*, London, England

# P is for Passion

Passion for an idea or concept is obviously important to kick start a business isn't it? But, how do you know you are passionate *enough*? We all have lots of ideas. How do you know which one to go for? Consider what you loved to do as a child. Do you have a recurring dream? Or does a new idea fire you up every time you talk about it? Can you feel the energy? That's passion.

Someone would ask me do you love running your business? Yes I do. I love it. I'm so passionate about it. I would say to any woman who's going to go down that road, be passionate about it. Because I sit here at 11 o'clock at night writing e-mails and doing stuff. That's because I want to and because I know it's for me, it's for my benefit.

Naz Lewis, Back2work Mum,
*www.back2workmum.co.uk*, Surrey, England

I sold the business just before we adopted Rosie and I actually intended being a full time mum but... this passion appeared. I honestly didn't expect it to; I thought right, that's great. I can retire now. By retiring, I mean, I'm going to be a mum now like my mum was. Mums have changed and moved on, and to be a mum is great, there's nothing wrong with it, but I think a lot of women need more. And I think if they become passionate about something, it's possible to do both well.

Anne Ryan, Handbag Heaven,
*www.handbagheaven.ie*, Dublin, Ireland

> It's essential. If you're not passionate about it, forget it!
>
> Sian Maloney, Gifts and Vouchers,
> *www.giftsandvouchers.ie*,
> Co. Meath, Ireland

> Looking into the future as a 50-year-old woman I still felt incredibly excited about my business. And I think what's really important when new mums are thinking of new ideas is that they should try and think far into the future, and see if the passion could still be there in or 20 years' time.
>
> Vicki Knights, Family Photographer,
> *www.vickiknights.co.uk*, London, England

> I wanted to make a difference. I thought, I can do this. I can really create something that will have a long lasting impact on the world, on the planet. 'Here you go, Jill's trying to save the planet' is what everybody used to say to me. So I ended up becoming passionate about it because I could see that I was making a difference.
>
> Jill Barker, Green Baby,
> *www.greenbaby.co.uk*, London, England

I was thinking about having a baby and I was thinking I don't want to be 70 and look back and think I had this really interesting idea, I wonder what would have happened? It just felt like the right time to go for it. I think you do have to be passionate because there are so many hurdles to clear and cynics you meet along the way The fact that we are so possessive about our customer service really helps drive things along. If you feel passionately that there is a certain way of doing things, then it's a lot easier to make sure that that happens.

Sophie Devonshire, Babes With Babies, *www.babeswithbabies.com*, London, England

I think we were very lucky when we launched Nappy Valley that the green issues were at the top of everyone's agenda. I cannot bear waste, and I never really got why everyone wanted to buy everything new when you could re-use perfectly good items. I'm still really passionate about that. I want to try and encourage people to follow that philosophy and stop buying everything new when there's so much out there that can be re-used. I've always been passionate about people finding a good deal.

Joanna Pearce, Nappy Valley, *www.nappyvalley.co.uk*, London and Guildford, England

You have to believe in your product and we knew that our product would make a genuine difference to every single day of life with a new baby... and also, as soon as you start to get feedback, it's incredible. We're two and a half years down the line now but we still get customer e-mails telling us how much this simple product has made a difference to the life of a family with a new baby, it's fantastic and it really drives you because, you know, you have a product that people are genuinely enjoying, which is lovely.

Ultimately, it's also about making money and our intention is to make enough money to have options available for our children. As working mums, we earned our own money. To us it's very important to be achieving that for our kids and so that is a huge motivating factor.

Helen Wooldridge, Cuddledry,
*www.cuddledry.com*, Somerset, England

The passion part is extremely important. I've seen so many businesses built out of passion and hobbies for simple things. I mean, you want to enjoy doing it and after all you're creating your business, this is your one opportunity to create the business that suits you, that you want absolutely. So find something that you're passionate about.

Darina Loakman, I am a WAHM,
*www.iamawahm.com*, Dublin, Ireland

Having studied psychology and knowing that I wanted to work with children gave me the passion to develop Musical Minis. What I found important was to focus the passion and turn it into determination and drive. I'm not very creative, so I didn't have a whole load of ideas to run with unlike some people really so I decided to follow my instincts. You do have to be passionate about your ideas if you want them to succeed. It's got to be passion that's driving you, something you really want for your children.

Karen Sherr, Musical Minis,
*www.musicalminis.co.uk*, Middlesex, England

The ideas, they haunt you until you start doing something. I'd wake up, or not even be able to get to sleep in the first place, because I had these ideas going around my head. You think: OK, I want to try and do something about this... I live and breathe it. For me, it's a natural flow through. I think if you're not able to sleep at night because these ideas aren't going away, you've got to do something about them. That's the passion!

Karen Simmonds, Travel Matters,
*www.travelmatters.co.uk*, London, England

I think that the trick about the passion is that it doesn't necessarily mean that you have to be passionate about the thing you are doing. It sounds really weird, but, for example, I've always been quite disparaging about being what the industry generally describes as a 'PR lovey darling'. I completely and utterly get the importance of public relations, it's a no-brainer, it is the most cost-effective tool for small companies to get their name out there, and it is far more effective than advertising and a lot of other marketing. So I truly believe that PR works. But if you ever ask me if doing public relations completely and utterly lights my fire and fills me with passion – no, it probably doesn't, but where my passion comes from is that I want to be able to create something, a lifestyle and a business that I can work around my children. I wanted something that would give me the flexibility to be there for them, at the same time allowing me to be creative.

Melissa Talago, PeekaBoo Communications,
www.peekaboocoms.co.uk, Berkshire, England

I know Anna often talks about being motivated by making a difference, and that certainly counts a great deal for me too. Making a difference which you can really sense whether you're approaching a woman over the telephone or you're working with a group of managers in a room or group maternity coaching where people are having conversations that they simply haven't been able to have in the workplace before. You can't help but feel passionate. It's very, very inspiring.

Jennifer Liston-Smith, Managing Maternity Ltd
*www.managingmaternity.co.uk*, Llanelwy, Wales

It's funny because I can't wait to read your book. Because it's exactly what I've been looking for, because ever since I started out with this I'm like but how do I know, how do I know if I'm really passionate about this. What's the difference between me and someone who is doing it? How do you know when you're actually doing it? How do you know if you're passionate enough about it? I had four or five ideas I was working on. I was passionate about all of them because I wanted to do anything to stop going back to work. Anything that keeps me home and gives me more time the better. I decided on the pram covers. But it was great fun to work on all the different ideas and I think it has to be fun in the beginning. You have to really enjoy working on it. And I think if you start getting bored with your idea or it annoys you or it feels like a duty, then you should leave it. It has to be fun and interesting for you to work on it all the time. I really love working on this and give as much time as I can possibly muster to work on it, I enjoy every second. Because I know it's getting me somewhere and I really believe in it.

Birgitte Lydum, Baby Beamers,
*www.babybeamers.com*, London, England

# A is for Action

That's where many of us come unstuck. We have passionate ideas and then nothing. The moment passes. What makes the difference between having an idea or a dream and having a business? Take action every day, one small step at a time. Go out and start asking questions, surf the internet, make a few phone calls. It does not matter what you do.. start. Start the ball rolling and as it rolls it will gain momentum propelling you forward.

> I think it's starting an action, a simple action. It might be as simple as buying a new work pen.
>
> Procrastinating is not going to work, and then if it's something that you're passionate about, you will find it easier to take the action. And once you do, the next one follows and the next one follows that.
>
> Darina Loakman, I am a WAHM, *www.iamawahm.com*, Dublin, Ireland

> I would have preferred to have stayed at home to be a mum but I was getting a little bit bored, you know. My brain was ticking over, I was driving my family demented, coming up with different business ideas all the time. So, eventually, enough was enough. I said right, time to put money where my mouth was. I came up with a business and I said 'I'm going to go with this one'. I did a lot of research into it and decided it was a runner! When I started working on it I was in hospital and I did my business plan and wrote it out and booked the domain name from my hospital bed!
>
> Sian Maloney, Gifts and Vouchers, *www.giftsandvouchers.ie*, Co. Meath, Ireland

I will know I've got to send an invoice to somebody and spend more time thinking about the fact that I've got to send it than it actually takes me to type up the invoice, PDF it and e-mail it.

Well it doesn't have to be right and perfect for you to go out and do something, get started, get stuck in, rather than thinking about it and wondering if you should get on with it. I asked somebody the other day who's been talking about all sorts of different businesses for I don't know how long 'what are you waiting for? 'Oh well, I've got to do this and that, I don't know, I want it to be the right time. Well, what is the right time? How do you know what the right time is?

Natalie Lue, London, England,
Self Employed Mum (*www.selfemployedmum.co.uk*),
Baggage Reclaim (*www.baggagereclaim.co.uk*),
Bambino Goodies (*www.bambinogoodies.co.uk*),
Nest Goodies (*www.nestgoodies.co.uk*)

I think for me it was talking about it because I felt I wanted to. I was upset that I couldn't do my job as I did before. I loved my job but I was away from home about eight months out of 12 and I couldn't do it with my baby. So I started talking to people about this idea I had and I think what spurred me on was the reaction I had from other people. I'd talk to anyone, even sitting on the bus, about the idea and people would say 'Wow that's a really good idea', or 'I don't know anyone else who does that. That's a brilliant idea.'

I'd advise anyone to talk and talk even if you're not doing it yet. Talk as if you're doing it and things will happen!

Rita Kobrak, Mums to Italy,
*www.mum-and-baby-experience.vpweb.co.uk*, London, England

I was beginning to twiddle my fingers a little bit and then, I set on the idea and thought this is ridiculous, if I don't do it somebody else will. It also coupled with the fact that when we got back from holiday, there was a card inviting me as a woman to do an online course in enterprise, and so, I thought, well, why not? It's not going to cost me anything. So I signed up. They gave me £80 to test my business idea and that was enough to buy a logo, and was all it took to get me going.

Wendy Shand, Tots To Travel,
*www.totstotravel.co.uk*, Peterborough, England

No one really tells you how difficult, well sorry, everybody tells you how difficult it is having a baby, but we all know you don't believe them until you have one. I think I got very involved in the having a baby bit for a few months and didn't think about anything because I honestly couldn't. I didn't have time. My dad used to be in business too and he's retired, but his way of retiring is still pottering around doing bits and bobs. So he was researching it for me. After about six months he sent me all the information he had gathered about all these suppliers. So that bit was done. I then started to take action. He knew that I'd need something to do other than having a baby even though it was a full time job!

Anne Ryan, Handbag Heaven,
*www.handbagheaven.ie*, Dublin, Ireland

A friend and I agreed to do a nanny share one morning a week and she had a teaching job, and I don't really feel comfortable paying for someone to look after my baby. At first I was going to sit around and have coffee, so I thought, I'm paying so much to have my child looked after, I've got to do something. I had Tuesday morning free so the first Tuesday I registered the company name, the next Tuesday I opened a bank account and then I set up my meetings on all the Tuesdays and that really, really made me do it.

> Joanna Pearce, Nappy Valley, *www.nappyvalley.co.uk*,
> London and Guildford, England

I had to do something and it was the only thing I knew how to do. The only daunting thing for me was probably tiredness, but when you're a lot younger you don't think about that. You realise at two o'clock in the morning when you're still painting the tigers that actually you're quite tired! I think you get on with it, and if you allow yourself to be daunted then that will hold you back. I think it is a question of just doing it and using a lot of energy and keeping at it. I think that's one of the magic things - never give up.

> Sarah Sherrington, Illustrator, Sarah Sherrington Designs,
> *www.sarahsherrington.co.uk*, London, England

The first thing I did was to get the website up and running because I guess I felt like I needed a bit of credibility and I think that's what a lot of people feel when they have a website and when they have business cards. it helps make you feel like you are in business. That was definitely the case for me. You know, fake it till you make it.

Alli Price, Motivating Mum,
*www.motivatingmum.co.uk*, London, England

It's funny, the business has grown considerably over the past years and when you stand here and look back, people often think, oh yes, it was all this and the growth was really obvious. But actually when you're standing at the beginning of it it's not obvious at all. I really liked the idea of setting up a business and as I said, this friend and I had this boob idea. It wasn't like we had this idea and we thought, oh yes, it's going to turn into a multi million pound business. You don't really know with ideas. Everybody has ideas all the time and you can explore and research but until you actually go for it, you don't really know if it's actually going to work. I don't think there was any way anybody could tell at the beginning that it was going to be as successful and it was going to work as well as it has. I certainly couldn't.

Sarah Tremellen, Bravissimo,
*www.bravissimo.com*, Leamington Spa, England

Every time my son was sleeping, I was on the internet looking up everything, setting up my website. I started off offering my friends discounted rates to build my portfolio and then I became a member of a professional body so I knew my work was up to a good standard and my clients could be assured of professional service. And I launched it. I got my first enquiry through Google. I thought, my God! And then it went from there. I e-mailed every single mum I think I've ever said two words to and told them to tell all their friends I've started doing discounted rates. I try and get at least one referral from every single family I do, and obviously that then spirals.

Vicki Knights, Family Photographer,
*www.vickiknights.co.uk*, London, England

From our perspective, being involved in the coaching world you're talking with clients about how they can take steps to move things forward. I think it was about walking the talk in our case, as well as practising what we preach. It's around being very clear about what your outcome is and making sure you've got a plan in place. But I think it's also about bringing together ideas, and being very determined about things.

Anna Hayward, Managing Maternity Ltd,
*www.managingmaternity.co.uk*, East Sussex, England

We had to take the baby to all the interviews, and there I was, sitting opposite the bank manager with a baby on my knee. It kind of spurred me on a bit. I think I was a bit of a quitter before I had the baby, and when I had my first son, suddenly I couldn't give up. And it is difficult and it is tough and you can't say you won't do that anymore because you've got a baby and you're responsible for that child's life and the implications of dumping it are too enormous to even consider. So I found a kind of reliance in myself that I've never really known before.

At some point, you've got to take action and you've got to say OK, I will have a go at it and you don't ever really know what is going to happen and whether it's going to work till you actually take the big leap.

Sarah Tremellen, Bravissimo,
*www.bravissimo.com*, Leamington Spa, England

I say I've got so many ideas, there's not enough hours in the day. But people who don't take action are perhaps the type of people who like to tick things off lists. You know, answer all the questions. The problem is that if you sit down and write lists of all the problems that a potential business idea might present, you're unlikely to do it. You'll never get to the end of it because every question leads off to another 50 questions.

Wendy Shand, Tots To Travel,
*www.totstotravel.co.uk*, Peterborough, England

I love the saying that I'm eating an elephant: you can eat a whole elephant if you take it one bite at a time and I think that's very applicable to this. Know what your elephant is, know what your vision is and know what you want to achieve and then take it step by step by step. Getting it started was in lots of ways the hardest. I've got a very good book recommendation: *Start Your Business Week by Week* by Steve Parks and it's really simply written and really accessible. It helped me hugely because he breaks things down into bite-sized chunks and it gives you very much a sense of this is doable. So I recommend it to anyone who's having any problems with the action bit.

Sophie Devonshire, Babes With Babies,
*www.babeswithbabies.com*, London, England

I thought, well I would use it but I needed to find out if other people would use it and I decided to run the idea past other people. So I got friends of friends to create focus groups and I held two evenings with people who I didn't know. I didn't want people just sitting there going oh yes that's a wonderful idea just because they're my friends. I got independent people to come round and I'd created action concept boards, demonstrating how do people currently shop online, what kind of things are people looking for and then I presented the idea of the site and how this could work etc. I mean, it was definitely the best thing I could have done because on the plus side it reaffirmed that yes, there was a need for it, other people would use it but I suppose also on the plus side but slightly negative was a lot of my ideas were completely rubbished: the route I was going

> down and the packaging that I was thinking about and the whole layout didn't prove popular with them at all. I really took their comments on board and I'm so glad, it was just the best. You know, if you've got eight people sitting there all saying same the thing, you need to change something.
>
> Claire Wilson, Send A Thought,
> *www.sendathought.co.uk*, London, England

But even when the business is established there is still action required to ensure it grows. Karen Simmonds is broadening her agency along ethical tourism lines.

> It's a simple idea but it takes time and patience to get the wheels in motion. I've had to do quite a lot of market research. I've joined campaigns/charities, it's a slow process but I'm trying to build it up and make my clients aware how their holiday choices can make a difference to the country, to the families around the hotel. I'm only scratching the surface but it's a start and again it's something that will take a lot of time and will develop slowly and steadily but I think that if things are supposed to happen, doors open. You've got to be patient. I've learnt quite a lot in the past 10 years about being patient.
>
> Karen Simmonds, Travel Matters,
> *www.travelmatters.co.uk*, London, England

# R is for Relationships

I think for most people the main issue with setting up on your own are those three little words - on your own! It can be scary not to have the backup of a large corporation behind you. But you will be amazed at the number of people waiting to help you. From government agencies to friends and family, from business networking to social networking, from suppliers to customers- put yourself out there as you will find people who can advise and support you.

This is an area that I was probably the most concerned about. I used to say years ago, I could never work on my own. I worked for a large media company for over 10 years before having my little boy and everyone knew how much I thrived in that environment. I managed quite a big team as well. And I loved that, loved having meetings, loved having grown up talk and banter. So that was the one thing that made me think should I do this, should I not?

But whenever I get a text or an e-mail or phone call saying, 'Oh my God, Vicki, I've seen the gallery and it made me cry' I'm delighted. I get so much of a boost from that and you know, I'm lucky I have a job that gives people so much pleasure. That means so much more than a pat on the back from a boss. I didn't quite realise I would get that.

Vicki Knights, Family Photographer,
*www.vickiknights.co.uk*, London, England

I think with any business you do need somebody to bounce ideas off. I mean at Musical Minis originally I used to try it out on my children. You need somebody to know you're going down the right track. I think relationships are very important.

Karen Sherr, Musical Minis,
*www.musicalminis.co.uk*,
Middlesex, England

In terms of relationships, it's great, as you say, that we are a team because what happens is you draw from each other's strengths. Jennifer's real skill is standing up in front of a conference and being able to talk about what the issues are for women, and then for me, I can get on the telephone and talk to potential clients. That's where being a double act really does come into its own.

Anna Hayward, Managing Maternity Ltd,
*www.managingmaternity.co.uk*, East Sussex, England

I would say my parents-in-law have been invaluable. My own parents live quite a distance away so they can't help. I'm sure they would if they were here, but my in-laws do and they've been fantastic at helping with childcare. Which has meant that I could work when I needed to work. Particularly during the busier periods, such as Christmas.

Victoria Dixon, Enhance Me,
*www.enhance-me.com*, Orkney, Scotland

My immediate family were very, very supportive and I don't know where I would be without them and my mum and my sister and everybody helping me out with the kids. I couldn't have done it without them. It was an instinctive thing and, you know, I'm working hard and I'm hoping it is going to work out for us because I know that if it does it will benefit the whole family.

Debra McVicker, Hampton Blue,
*www.hamptonblue.co.uk*, Belfast, Northern Ireland

My husband is incredibly supportive because he has been self-employed for years, so he knows how difficult it is to run a business. There were nights when he was tying the ribbons as well, trying to get an order out or whatever for the jam business. He is a pure entrepreneur as well,

Tara McCormack, Cardmagical and Berry Wild Jam
*www.cardmagical.com*, Co. Cavan, Ireland

Again it's my family, my mum helped me with choices of things to buy. We look at the stuff together because she's quite creative. She also helped me package stuff up when it arrived or unpack it or put things in boxes. My husband was brilliant because he looked after Rosie whenever she needed looking after.

Another relationship which is a bit of a funny one I suppose, was with my bank... I had a brilliant relationship with my bank to start with. Not only did I get free banking, but I also got two parties which were really, really successful and have generated subsequent sales and everybody knows me when I go into the branch and they all know Rosie and it's brilliant. A really, really good relationship and that was one that you wouldn't expect to have. Banks aren't exactly known for their friendliness.

Anne Ryan, Handbag Heaven,
*www.handbagheaven.ie*, Dublin, Ireland

Most of my suppliers are still the same ones I had 10 years ago. They're the ones who were involved in the growth so maybe that's one of the key things about making your business successful. It's actually starting from day one with suppliers that you can trust and work with whether that's getting catalogues designed or IT or anything like that. The whole thing has got to be finding people who are core to your business and they help you along the way.

Jill Barker, Green Baby,
*www.greenbaby.co.uk*, London, England

The IT firm that I chose to build the website - the guy who ran it was great. He bounced with ideas. He'd set up various small companies so he had lots of ideas to help me and I think that was my biggest support. I also joined some mums' networking groups. We would meet once a month and I'd have a brain storming session or there'd be a speaker. I found that really invaluable as well. It can be incredibly lonely working on your own.

Joanna Pearce, Nappy Valley, *www.nappyvalley.co.uk*, London and Guildford, England

I think the thing about Internet forums in particular is that women can go on to them and they are anonymous or virtually anonymous. They're not judged by their appearance or what car they drive and so therefore women can feel like they can ask for advice without being laughed at or judged in any manner and I think that's why the web site has been quite a success so far.

But my husband really is my greatest supporter. I think I surprised him and it's been lovely to hear him say actually, you know, I'm really proud of you, which I don't think he's said before.

Hannah Young, Scot Mum, *www.scotmum.com*, Edinburgh, Scotland

Our husbands have been pretty good. We have had to have their support and acceptance of what we're doing and that we're working all night, you know, juggling lives generally. The relationship between the two of us is very important and whether you work on your own or with a business partner can depend very much on who you are as a person and also in your personal situation. Polly and I took a decision at the beginning that it's important to work as a team because we are still part-timers. We've got very young kids and so by having two of us, it's like having one full time person, but it means we can still be good mummies - we're there to pick them up from school, we're around with our kids on the days when there's no child care but we're able to cover the business on a full time basis between us.

Helen Wooldridge, Cuddledry,
*www.cuddledry.com,* Somerset, England

Actually, I have this entire virtual world of other people. My husband was very supportive which I think is critical and I think if I've seen other people slightly pulled by the wayside, it's because they haven't got the support of a partner. My husband's got a skill set that's very different from mine and so we come together and have something that's quite special. I need his skills.

Wendy Shand, Tots To Travel,
*www.totstotravel.co.uk*, Peterborough, England

We also had a lot of support from our husbands. I think if you don't have the support of your family, it must be incredibly difficult because setting up a business is time consuming. It kind of consumes you as well. It takes over everything and actually Mike helped in practical terms, in buying, putting together some computer stuff as well as with some of our processes, but he also helped in terms of being there to encourage us and to say I'm behind you, which was really positive as well.

Sarah Tremellen, Bravissimo,
*www.bravissimo.com*, Leamington Spa, England

Relationships are important but it's also important not to rely on others too much on day-to-day aspects, because it is my initiative, and I am the one who's going to be driving and running this business, so it's not fair to drag everyone in. I think a support role is different from an active participation role and I have learnt a bit of a lesson there. They have their commitments as well.

Rita Derkatsch Nagy, Ming-Cha Tea,
*www.ming-cha.co.uk*, London, England

I only became a single mum in November of last year. But before then, I would have to say that my partner wasn't supportive of the business anyway. It's funny that you said that lots of mums have said their husbands are really supportive because lots of business mums that I've come across said that their husbands aren't at all. Which I think is something important to mention. I've found that a lot of husbands, because they're so money-focused, find it very difficult to understand what their wives are doing because they're not bringing in that much money. Lots of mums in business are only doing it because they really enjoy it and it's creative.

If women are lucky enough to have a supportive husband, one that really understands what they're doing and supports them that's so amazing and they should be so thankful because it's difficult when you don't have a husband that understands because then it's a constant battle. You never feel like you've got that person behind you.

Alli Price, Motivating Mum,
*www.motivatingmum.co.uk*, London, England

The process of setting up my own business made me re-evaluate a lot of relationships and made me realise how amazing my friends and family are. The other thing that's great is networking. That's been a real help. I've been writing to business women I've met or women who work for themselves and I've made some very, very good friends. We can call each other up in the middle of the day and say, 'I'm juggling with this, what do you think?' Or 'how do you manage this?' And that's been brilliant because also any time one of us is going 'this is really hard,' there's somebody else there. I definitely recommend for anyone who's doing it, to look into networking. It's a horrible word but it's all about finding new relationships. A virtual team, if you like.

Sophie Devonshire, Babes With Babies,
*www.babeswithbabies.com*, London, England

---

Luckily, I knew a few other mums who run their own business. They are a great support to me and we get together from time to time to brainstorm, share and support one another and I think it is important for all Mumpreneurs who are starting out to join Mumpreneur or women's business groups in order to find other individuals to help them in these ways. My best friend was also a PR advisor and he helped me with press releases, learning about exposure, and his enthusiasm for my ideas was infectious. I would say in terms of relationships, keep family and friends close to you during this time. It can be easy to get swept away and isolate yourself.

Monic Joint, Mummy Must Have,
*www.mummymusthave.com*, Southampton, England

In the early stages, I would say having a good Business Link advisor is very important. Having someone at the other end of the phone who you can contact and say, oh my God, this has gone wrong, what do we do now? You know, somebody who can help you see around the problem is very important. And for us, from the word go, we built up some very, very important relationships with other people within our industry who were already established. We were able to build friendships and learn from their advice. People who have already had successes or made mistakes and are willing to share. When you do ask for advice, people are willing to share, they really are.

Helen Wooldridge, Cuddledry,
*www.cuddledry.com,* Somerset, England

As woman, we sort of generally interested in knowing about what people are doing and supporting them. I know that a lot of women, depending on their businesses, a lot of them have grown through referrals and through networking and it's just amazing. And I think with the internet with Facebook and with things like that it's sort of just ready for women to say yes I can do this!

Naz Lewis, Back2work Mum,
*www.back2workmum.co.uk,* Surrey, England

# K is for Knowing

In Gemma's story she scribbles the word against her SPARKLES acronym without really knowing why.

She thinks she must really mean *knowledge* but knowledge can be brought in or acquired. If you don't know, ask someone who does, right?

*Knowing* is different. Knowing is about having faith, trusting your instincts and gut feelings. Forget all the excuses in your head; what is your heart saying? Does this idea feel right? Listen to these feelings and trust them.

I don't think we've ever completely wanted to give up. I think we knew that this was going to work from the word go but we have faced massive obstacles which have left us in tears at times but I think that inner knowledge that we have something here that could really succeed has always motivated us to continue and find a way around any obstacle.

Helen Wooldridge, Cuddledry,
*www.cuddledry.com*, Somerset, England

I think part of the problem is that we weave between over-analysing or under-thinking. I talked to people about self-esteem and confidence and trusting instinct and gut quite a bit and actually the best way to learn how to trust your instincts and your guts is to do it...because that's how you build up your confidence.

Natalie Lue, London, England,
Self Employed Mum (*www.selfemployedmum.co.uk*)

I think it's natural that you should have some moments of doubt but I think, when you get those, you need to weigh them up against how you really have made a difference in different settings, be it at the most senior board level or with an individual woman, and her relationship with her baby or her young family, so it's about being able to know when it's right to have doubts and accept that that's part of the process.

Anna Hayward, Managing Maternity Ltd,
*www.managingmaternity.co.uk*, East Sussex, England

---

I think a gut instinct is very important. But that doesn't mean to say that sometimes it can't be wrong. And I think you have to know how long you're going to trust your gut instinct for if it keeps going wrong. There comes a point when perhaps your gut needs restringing.

I have a gut instinct that eventually the linen will succeed, but it's not only that. You look around and see lots of other shops, lots of other bed linen manufacturers suddenly producing children's embroidered bed linen. Things that haven't been around before and I know it wasn't when I started this so, I know that I'm on to a good thing.

Sarah Sherrington, Illustrator, Sarah Sherrington Designs,
*www.sarahsherrington.co.uk*, London, England

In the past, certainly when I was starting out, I would ignore my own gut feeling and go with what everybody else said. And there were times when that was absolutely the right thing to do and there were times when I regretted it. Even to this day, I struggle with this. But now I take a different approach, and you know, if I'm getting the opposite kind of reaction to the one I had expected but, in my gut, I know this is right. I won't necessarily go with them but I will stop and re-evaluate. I know that if in a day or two, I'm still not happy, then I will go with my own feeling. I'm learning to trust my instincts more than I did.

Darina Loakman, I am a WAHM,
*www.iamawahm.com*, Dublin, Ireland

That's one of the most frustrating things that you go through. You ask other people for their opinions and although it's very nice for people to give their opinions it can end up being the most confusing thing you do when it comes to the actual decision making. I remember sending out to a group of 10 friends saying which logo do you prefer and there was a choice of five logos and everyone came back with different choices. Sometimes just asking for too many opinions and not going with your gut feeling is a downfall. So I quickly learnt that actually there are some things that you just need to make the call on. It's your business, it's your decision, as long as you've got the general go ahead on the idea from other people, the details needs to come down to you.

Claire Wilson, Send A Thought,
*www.sendathought.co.uk*, London, England

There came a time when I was doing my research, when I really, really believed that I could do this and I knew myself. I started trusting myself more and started getting more of my confidence back that I had lost from being on maternity leave because I think that happens to most women. They stop believing in themselves and they forget what they are good at. I think, as you said, at some point in that process of researching the business I got to the point where I knew I could do this and whether I did it on my own or whether my sister joined me or, but it didn't really matter.

Debra McVicker, Hampton Blue,
*www.hamptonblue.co.uk*, Belfast, Northern Ireland

You have to go a little bit with your gut and trust that and speak to people and hope that you've got the right idea. Listen to your instincts, especially as a new mum, because you know what you're looking for and if you're looking for it, there are going to be hundreds if not thousands of other mums looking for it as well.

Vicki Knights, Family Photographer,
*www.vickiknights.co.uk*, London, England

> When I was looking at your acronym, I too was looking at *knowing*. For me a really important thing is not knowing that your business is right, it's knowing when you're doing something right, to trust your gut instinct. There have been several occasions where I've had a problem. Someone who's approached me and I've thought I don't really want to work with them, and whenever I've ignored that gut instinct and gone ahead, there has invariably been a problem. And there have been times when I have asked for my husband's advice on something; he approaches any problem with a very corporate, masculine head, and it doesn't sit well with the way we operate as mothers. It's a completely different way of working and I find that I can take on board his advice and listen to it from a purely business point of view, but, I've got to listen to my own instinct.
>
> Melissa Talago, PeekaBoo Communications,
> www.peekaboocoms.co.uk, Berkshire, England

> I think even if it doesn't work straight away, something inside you tells you to keep going. But I'd had some other ideas, you know, thrown at me: so why don't you do this, why don't you do that, but I wasn't sure about them. There was something inside me thinking no that's not for me whereas this was something that I thought is going to work. It might take a while but it will work.
>
> Rita Kobrak, Mums to Italy,
> *www.mum-and-baby-experience.vpweb.co.uk*, London, England

I know that what Babes With Babies does is right. It's based on a genuine consumer insight on how mums feel and how happy flattering, lovely gifts can make them feel. I know the way we do it is right. We give great customer service. We care about choosing our products and do everything we can to make buying them a good experience, and I know we treat our suppliers with respect and our team works together very supportively. So, I've got this sense inside me that any success we've had is based on something strong.

Sophie Devonshire, Babes With Babies,
*www.babeswithbabies.com*, London, England

I think a lot of it has to do with intuition. A deep sense of knowing – I knew when we started that mums and dads need a good holiday. I knew they would want to go to a self-catering villa or apartment or something and I knew that they needed all the bits and pieces to make their life easier. There were bits I didn't know but we've answered those questions as we've gone along.

Wendy Shand, Tots To Travel,
*www.totstotravel.co.uk*, Peterborough, England

But even with a good idea, a successful business, you still need to keep listening to that inner voice.

> Oh God it's like grieving. I couldn't believe the orders stopped coming in and I knew six months ago that it was gone, my gut feeling was, yes, I really need to go and do something else. But it's hard to let go as well. It was kind of hard for me to accept that it was over, because I had put so much time and effort into it, but hopefully this other venture will take off.
>
> I think women usually are right when they go with their gut feeling. I know that's probably an old wives' tale. But I think generally we do know what's right and what's wrong and what to go for and what not to do.
>
> Tara McCormack, Cardmagical and Berry Wild Jam
> *www.cardmagical.com*, Co. Cavan, Ireland

## L is for Learning

When starting up you may be an expert in your field or just someone with a good idea. Whatever you think you know already you will find setting up a business, like becoming a mother, is the steepest of learning curves. From keeping accounts to sourcing suppliers, from marketing to database construction you will probably have to learn it all. But there are amazing services run by, for example:

- Business Link in England (*www.businesslink.gov.uk*)
- Business Gateway and Highlands and Islands Enterprise in Scotland (*www.bgateway.com* or *www.hie.co.uk*)
- Business Eye in Wales (*www.businesseye.org.uk*)
- Invest Northern Ireland in, you guessed it, Northern Ireland (*www.investni.com*)
- County & City Enterprise Boards in the Republic of Ireland (*www.enterpriseboards.ie*) where you can take free or very cheap courses on all the key subjects.

You should also contact your local Chamber of Commerce and don't forget the internet where you will find loads of forums, networking groups and business clubs (check out our website for links).

Like motherhood, no one can prepare you for the realities of having a child and it is the same in business. You cannot know everything at the beginning but will learn as you go. At times it will be daunting but it's part of the rich tapestry of life. Enjoy it!

The main thing I've learned is that a good idea is not enough. I have always thought that if you have good ideas they will automatically become successful. But that's not how it works. You really have to, work hard and you and you alone have to make all the preparations, do all the ground work and really promote it. There's a lot more involved than I thought. Even though it's quite a simple idea, I've been amazed sometimes why people don't jump up and down and say yes we'll buy 10,000 of these. It's not as easy as that. You need to have business sense as well. You need to know a lot of things about the different aspects of the business.

Birgitte Lydum, Baby Beamers,
*www.babybeamers.com*, London, England

I did think I would keep it all in-house and do it myself but the web site I produced was woeful and it wouldn't have attracted anybody. So I got somebody to design it for me. Sometimes I think letting go of control and asking for help is a big learning curve.

Hannah Young, Scot Mum,
*www.scotmum.com*, Edinburgh, Scotland

In a normal business situation, if you go into a normal corporate structure, you learn a lot from your boss. You learn a lot from other people. You learn and progress. If you're an entrepreneur, then that's not open to you. There is no boss, there is nobody there. Learn from others and seek advice but don't necessarily believe that what they've said is the way that you've got to do it for your business because nobody knows your business as you do. You've got to have a go yourself and learn what works.

Sarah Tremellen, Bravissimo,
*www.bravissimo.com*, Leamington Spa, England

You know, I've only been in business since November, 2008 but I found as a new business the support I got from other businesses was so helpful: explaining things – like I'm learning as I go along all the time. I've got wise in such a short space of time because people take time to teach me things and explain things and that's why I try to take time to pass it on if anybody asks me.

It's so enjoyable.

Sian Maloney, Gifts and Vouchers,
*www.giftsandvouchers.ie*, Co. Meath, Ireland

> I would say most importantly that the way you are going to learn is by doing. You could sit and buy a million books and read up on what you are supposed to do, but the best way to learn is to go and do it. And you will make mistakes along the way, but at least you will learn from these mistakes.
>
> Melissa Talago, PeekaBoo Communications,
> www.peekaboocoms.co.uk, Berkshire, England

> We've learnt that you do not need to know everything and you don't need to pretend you do, either. I think it's very easy to feel like you have to pretend you do. For example, say for us, when we were in a meeting with a major retailer and they came up with terminology we didn't understand, in the beginning we bluffed our way through which can leave you in an awkward situation, What we've learnt is that it doesn't matter. Nobody's going to care if you don't know. In fact I think it makes people warm to you a bit more.
>
> Helen Wooldridge, Cuddledry,
> *www.cuddledry.com,* Somerset, England

> Many women love to talk, even if it's typing away on a blog or forum. I think there's always going to be somebody who's going to give you bit of advice, good or bad, whether you take in on or not. The internet has changed the world. It's like having another member of the family sitting in the corner: you can ask them anything and they will answer back in some form.
>
> Tara McCormack, Cardmagical and Berry Wild Jam
> *www.cardmagical.com*, Co. Cavan, Ireland

Everything is learning for me. I enjoy learning anyway. You try to resolve it as best as you can. If you can't, then you try to get some help. My mum's Chinese and I was brought up in Hong Kong and I can read and write Chinese but I can't speak Mandarin which is what my supplier speaks. We cannot communicate by speaking to each other so I can't pick up the phone and go, 'hey Mr. Wu, where is my tea?' So I basically had to brush up my writing skills and on top of that to learn how to be able to produce Chinese characters on the computer so that I can e-mail him. That has been another great challenge but a very fun and interesting one.

Rita Derkatsch Nagy, Ming-Cha Tea,
*www.ming-cha.co.uk*, London, England

---

You know, the main things that I learned, I mean even regardless of jam, card, stationery, whatever, is, one, the value of your product, and, two, the value of your time.

Tara McCormack, Cardmagical and Berry Wild Jam
*www.cardmagical.com*, Co. Cavan, Ireland

---

I think probably, learning to listen. My mum used to tell me often, that I used to open my mouth much too soon, before I'd even thought about what I was saying and consequently I wasn't listening as well. I've learnt to *listen* to what other people are saying instead of thinking that I know the answer already. It was crucial and quite a steep learning curve to start with.

Karen Simmonds, Travel Matters,
*www.travelmatters.co.uk*, London, England

One of the best things about going through this process has been the fact that you're forced into learning these things. Sometimes, the learning might be painful and you might make mistakes but I think doing anything like this certainly feels like your brain is fully exercised and it is very exciting to realise the potential. For me the potential of the internet is terribly exciting. I'm glad I've learnt about that.

Sophie Devonshire, Babes With Babies,
*www.babeswithbabies.com*, London, England

I did actually do a business degree. I went back to college as a mature student, only because I realised that leaving school too early had been a bad thing. So I went and got my degree in business but I don't actually think you ever really use what you learn in university. As much as people who write the books like to think that you will practise that in real life, you don't. Real life doesn't work like that. You can get some of your ideas from books but at the end of the day, you have to roll with what goes on. You can't refer to a book every time something goes wrong. You only have to watch Dragon's Den to see that people become multi-millionaires without any qualifications whatsoever. So, I definitely think that shouldn't put anybody off doing anything.

Anne Ryan, Handbag Heaven,
*www.handbagheaven.ie*, Dublin, Ireland

You need to have an umbrella, an overview, of what's going on, of what you need to learn but you don't need to get into the nitty gritty. There's always somebody who can do it or help you with it. So I suppose it's being a farmer, for instance; you don't have to be that cow making the milk but you do need to have to know that a cow delivers milk and know how to milk the cow.

Darina Loakman, I am a WAHM,
*www.iamawahm.com*, Dublin, Ireland

Another learning tip you need very early on is to make sure you've got backup. If some of my children were ill, I needed somebody to step in and either help with the business or look after the children. If you don't you learn very quickly that you're in trouble.

Karen Sherr, Musical Minis,
*www.musicalminis.co.uk*, Middlesex, England

You know, success doesn't come easily or cheaply. If you're really going to go for it, don't feel you are just investing in a business. You're investing in yourself, and if you create something fantastic, not only are you going to have something to show to those around you but your children are going to take their cue from you one day too and say, look mummy did it! She had little kids at home and she went out there and she created this for herself and it's a really worthwhile venture. The sky's the limit. Never put a limit on the height of the sky.

Monic Joint, Mummy Must Have,
*www.mummymusthave.com*, Southampton, England

I feel I've learnt quite a lot from the women I coach. I'm thinking about somebody I've recently been coaching and she was talking about how she was feeling, you know, that she had not fully given herself credit for some of her achievements in the past, and now was feeling a lack of confidence. Women can be very hard task masters in terms of their own career and I think one of the things I've learnt from the women I've been coaching is to focus on what it is that you do well rather than focus on all the other things that you haven't yet managed to do or you would like to do.

Anna Hayward, Managing Maternity Ltd,
*www.managingmaternity.co.uk*, East Sussex, England

(After 10 years) you still have to keep learning and you still have to make sure you don't shelter yourself away. I think sometimes companies do that. They get so busy. Some of the smaller companies box themselves away day to day and they forget to go out there and network and speak to people, and attend fairs and conferences and stuff like that because there's still stuff you need to learn.

Jill Barker, Green Baby,
*www.greenbaby.co.uk*, London, England

# E is for Enthusiasm

In the book we call enthusiasm energy in human form. Without it nothing gets done. It's contagious and it's vital to getting any idea off the ground. Knowing your idea is good and believing in yourself and your product/service is vital to the success of any business.

You have to love what you do.

If you do not, why should anyone else? You will be amazed at what that love can achieve. The first few months of a newborn's life is filled with sleepless nights and smelly nappies and at times it seems impossible to cope. But if you keep faith and keep the energy moving forward these difficult times will pass. Your loving efforts will be rewarded by a smile or a hug which makes it all worthwhile. Now you may not get hugs from your customers but if you have a great product /service and you lovingly persist through the hard times you will begin to get referrals, return business and perhaps even a thank you.

Well I think the enthusiasm, for me, goes with the enjoyment. I think it's impossible to have one without the other, and I really enjoyed watching the business develop and grow as I did watching my children develop and grow. And that doesn't mean there aren't days when either the children or the business have got me down, but overall there are a lot more good days than there are bad days and I wouldn't give the children up and I wouldn't give the business up.

Karen Sherr, Musical Minis,
*www.musicalminis.co.uk*, Middlesex, England

Becoming a mother, I had to knuckle down and get on with it and it gave me a resilience that I have used massively in business since. There are times when you're so tired, particularly when you've got children and you just keep going. I have had to work through the night many times because that's the only time I had when I didn't have children around but the resilience keeps you going and I don't think I learnt that until I had a baby.

Sarah Tremellen, Bravissimo,
*www.bravissimo.com*, Leamington Spa, England

I think it's like running. You start running one kilometre and you quite enjoy it, and something spurs you on to one and a half then you do two. It all goes together. I don't think there's any one rule, if you enjoy it, the more you do the more you can do, and the more you learn and the fewer mistakes you start to make.

Sarah Sherrington, Illustrator, Sarah Sherrington Designs,
*www.sarahsherrington.co.uk*, London, England

It's amazing how a few months of unpaid maternity leave can fill you with enthusiasm! A shortage of cash in our household was a great contributor to my enthusiasm when I started childminding. I had to make a success of it, simply because we needed the money!

Karen Muxworthy,
*www.karenmuxworthy.com*,
Freedom Events, *www.freedomevents-sussex.com*

> You will come up across so many obstacles that if you don't have the enthusiasm, you're not going to get over them.
>
> Darina Loakman, I am a WAHM,
> *www.iamawahm.com*, Dublin, Ireland

> Well, my mind's always bursting with ideas. I find I've always got new ideas for the business, and it's just a lack of time more than anything. But being a mum obviously is a full time job and I feel completely worn out at times. But I find that when I feel a lack of enthusiasm, I network and even just chatting online to other mums who might be in the same position, or updating my blog or going on Twitter always lifts my spirits and I quite often need that feeling of being inspired.
>
> Victoria Dixon, Enhance Me,
> *www.enhance-me.com*, Orkney, Scotland

> I love the aspect of being able to work at home and run the business at home and be a mum at the same time. It's fantastic. I'm enjoying it.
>
> Sian Maloney, Gifts and Vouchers,
> *www.giftsandvouchers.ie*, Co. Meath, Ireland

I make lists all the time. I make lists of little steps along the way to the fulfilment of each goal. And if I'm having a particularly difficult day one of the things I do is pick one of the easier steps from my list. Last week my daughter forgot how to sleep for three nights so by the third morning I was on my knees. I knew that my concentration wasn't 100% so on a day like that, I do small things like ringing the Post Office to find out how much it would cost to post a book... I pick things that don't require so much concentration. And the other thing is to make a list of things you really enjoy that don't cost anything.

I really enjoy watching the robins. They come and they hop on my clothes line. I know it's very a small, very simple thing but I will make a point at breakfast of waiting and watching them and giving myself a few minutes to realise, you know, that I will get a night's sleep at some stage and slow myself down like that. I find those things work for me and I remind myself why I'm doing this, because if only one person reads the book and realises that they can actually make their lives a happy place then my joy is complete.

Martine Brennan, Contented Living Publishing and Coaching, *www.contentedlliving.com* and Author of *Happiness It's Just A Habit, www.happinessitsjustahabit.com*, Co. Kerry, Ireland

What I love about what I do is I feel like I have two different roles. I've got my mummy role and my career role. My day is so varied. And so I'm enthusiastic because it's so different all the time. I'll go from doing a 60th birthday party one day to a newborn shoot with gorgeous little curled up hands and feet the next day. I want them to be 100% satisfied and delighted with everything. So that gives me the enthusiasm.

Vicki Knights, Family Photographer,
*www.vickiknights.co.uk*, London, England

My enthusiasm was very much tied to my dreams of getting my business and parenting writing off the ground. The dreams I had fed the energy really. I never stopped eating, preening, sleeping my dreams for my business, for myself. The dreams were the fuel I needed to turn them into reality. You know, don't let anyone or anything sway you. If you believe what you have is something amazing to offer, keep getting your message across. Define your dreams clearly to yourself and to others. Enthusiasm is infectious. If you believe in yourself, so will other people whether that's your friend, your family or anyone else that's involved in the business world.

Monic Joint, Mummy Must Have,
*www.mummymusthave.com*, Southampton, England

One of the images in my head is sitting on GMTV talking to somebody about my business. You just keep seeing that in your head and keep saying I'm going to get that. I'm going to do that one day and you'll see that it's that kind of thing that keeps you going.

Naz Lewis, Back2work Mum,
*www.back2workmum.co.uk*, Surrey

But what about money?

The way I see it is you can't think about the money side of it straight away. That will come later. You have to give before you get back anything and if someone thinks about the money without any passion for what they're doing then it's not going to work. If you have the passion and enthusiasm then the money will eventually come.

Rita Kobrak, Mums to Italy,
*www.mum-and-baby-experience.vpweb.co.uk*, London, England

I would say is that for me one of the things about having children in terms of motivation and enthusiasm for business is that money takes on a whole new meaning. I've always been somebody who finds it hard to be motivated by money, in and of itself. I never really got that very much until I had children. Obviously, everything one wants to do with children costs money and because I have responsibility for a family and their future, I find that very motivating in a business sense because one has to keep going. I don't have the luxury that might have been there, you know, back in my early 20s.

Jennifer Liston-Smith, Managing Maternity Ltd
*www.managingmaternity.co.uk*, Llanelwy, Wales

But enthusiasm is infectious the more of it you have the more people will be drawn to your service or product.

> Obviously creating enthusiasm about yourself and what you sell is part of it. That's what people buy into.
>
> Natalie Lue, London, England, Self Employed Mum (*www.selfemployedmum.co.uk*)

But enthusiasm can be hard work...

> I don't push myself too hard. I don't know if this makes sense or not but I find that if you have absolutely no energy left at the end of the day, you won't produce good work. It becomes self-defeating and a waste of time in some cases. I guess one of the ways for me is that I realise that I'm much more of a morning person than realised I was, so I am more reliable, happier, enthusiastic, efficient if I get up at 5:00 in the morning, put in two hours before I get the children up, than I would say if I started at 8:00, 9:00, 10:00 at night. So the enthusiasm is very much maintained by focussing on the long-term prospects of having a success, but also I am seeing smaller results that we are hitting targets for and if I don't get too tired, everything keeps rolling.
>
> Rita Derkatsch Nagy, Ming-Cha Tea, *www.ming-cha.co.uk*, London, England

I think I've reached that point where I realise, OK everything takes 10 times longer than before I had the baby. And that's fine, because it's worth it. In the beginning I would say, Oh God, I'll never get this done. But then I realised I have to accept these ups and downs. And what always gets me up again is talking to other mums. And it works every time. And it's literally calling one of them and talking to them and then I'm all at peace about it again afterwards.

Birgitte Lydum, Baby Beamers,
*www.babybeamers.com*, London, England

I don't know how you keep the enthusiasm, that's always there and so is the passion for it. I'm sure that there are times when you do think, gosh, can I keep doing this every day but that's still something you have got to really love, the business that you've started, haven't you? Love what you're doing. Make it fun. Make your work fun.

Jill Barker, Green Baby,
*www.greenbaby.co.uk*, London, England

I'm not what you would call a natural mother. I'm one of those mums who enjoys time away from their child. No, I was never ever born to be a stay-at-home mum and I find it very trying and difficult at times. You know, spending long periods of time with my daughter, because it's not what I was born for. To tell you the truth, the energy and the enthusiasm I get from going to these lunches is important because that is what I was born to do. I feel I'm not working. I'm like having a break. I'm having fun. As long as I can keep that balance between work and my daughter, that's great but if I ever lost the business and I was at home all the time, I know I would have no energy or enthusiasm. Yeah, so for me it's like my social vice. I love it.

Alli Price, Motivating Mum,
*www.motivatingmum.co.uk*, London, England

## S is for Self Belief

In our story Gemma has a real problem believing in herself, especially after the birth. Many of us experience baby blues or worse. We are often our own worst critics. A thousand people can tell you they believe in you but they are wasting their breath if you do not believe in yourself. Each and every one of us is unique. You are now a mother. There is at least one person in your world now who loves you unconditionally and relies on you for everything. They don't just think you are special, they are not saying it to make you feel better or to get you to work harder. *They know you are great and believe you can do anything – and they're right!*

I think after having Poppy I lost all my confidence and I didn't really know that might happen to me. I looked in the mirror one day and felt that the person looking back at me wasn't the old me and so I thought I needed to change my appearance. I got a radical new haircut and colour and new clothes and it gave me a boost and a bit more confidence because I felt like I was somebody.

Hannah Young, Scot Mum,
*www.scotmum.com*, Edinburgh, Scotland

---

If you don't believe in yourself then you're not going to take that step forwards and it's not all about having the money to create a product or you know, to do the marketing or whatever because I mean most people only start locally anyway. If it works then you'll go to the next step where you might get bigger. But you know, you have to have vision and you have to have a plan and if you don't have that well then, you know you may as well, as you say, go to school in your slippers.

Tara McCormack, Cardmagical and Berry Wild Jam
*www.cardmagical.com*, Co. Cavan, Ireland

---

The whole SPARKLES acronym is very good actually because it's not each individual letter, I think it's a combination of all of them, so in this S you need to encompass everything. You have to have the enthusiasm. You know, you need to learn that if you do these steps and know what you want to do, then that will help with your self-belief. The only thing I can say with that is you need to surround yourself with positive people.

Darina Loakman, I am a WAHM,
*www.iamawahm.com*, Dublin, Ireland

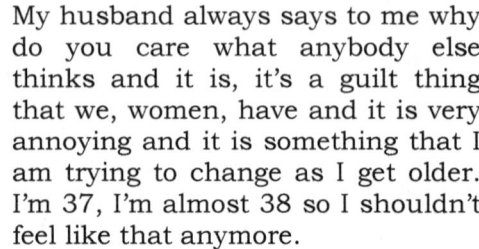

My husband always says to me why do you care what anybody else thinks and it is, it's a guilt thing that we, women, have and it is very annoying and it is something that I am trying to change as I get older. I'm 37, I'm almost 38 so I shouldn't feel like that anymore.

I think when you have a really bad day you have to sit down with a good friend who's known you for a long time, somebody who is level headed and maybe they have to remind you of what you used to be like and what you have achieved in your life You know a good pat on the back doesn't do anybody any harm, every now and again.

Debra McVicker, Hampton Blue,
*www.hamptonblue.co.uk*, Belfast, Northern Ireland

My self esteem and self belief used to be very poor. When we had adopted Rosie at the beginning of this business. I went to classes for assertiveness and self esteem building. Two nights before I was going to have a handbag party at my house I was like, 'I'm going to cancel, I'm going to cancel, but on the Saturday when my party was, all of the neighbours, people who I had never met before, came. All of my friends came, they'd driven from other parts of the city, people that you didn't expect to come. I did over €1000 in my house in a couple of hours!

Anne Ryan, Handbag Heaven,
*www.handbagheaven.ie*, Dublin, Ireland

I'm in the middle of doing this and I'm talking to manufacturers at the moment. So, at this point obviously I don't know if anything is going to come of it. But I'm quite sure it will and I'm hopeful that it will. I think the idea of becoming the next generation made me think that I needed to do something about all these ideas I always had. I think becoming a mum made me realise that I could do so much more than I had imagined. Because it was so much harder than I thought it would be, and so all of a sudden I realised, that the impossible is actually possible. And you can stay awake three nights in a row and still function somehow. All these things made me realise that I'm capable of much more than I thought I would be. That spurred me on.

Birgitte Lydum, Baby Beamers,
*www.babybeamers.com*, London, England

Life changes when you have a baby and you may decide to be an amazing full time mother and when you do it, you do it well or you may decide you want to do something else as well and learn a lot along the way, but it's believing that it's worth giving it a go and there isn't a reason why you shouldn't see it through. I think there are enough role models out there, enough examples of people from all kinds of backgrounds, all types of people who can succeed, and if people do look at role models and research it, I think they can believe it's possible. But the question is more, is it right for you? Is that what fits into your life? Is it what fits in with what you want to do?

Sophie Devonshire, Babes With Babies,
*www.babeswithbabies.com*, London, England

I really feel for new mums particularly, because I think there are so many people telling them, you must do this, you must do that,. And what makes me laugh is, if they're men writing a book, those men were not at home with their babies when they were little. But even women writing the books, they weren't at home with their children when they were little either. They were also doctors or psychologists or they were doing something else.

Martine Brennan, Contented Living Publishing and Coaching, *www.contentedliving.com* and Author of *Happiness It's Just A Habit, www.happinessitsjustahabit.com*, Co. Kerry, Ireland

Don't be scared. It's very easy to think it's my own business. Things could go wrong and it could be embarrassing. It could cost me loads of money. Don't think about that. I think you need to think: Let me look at my future if I don't start this business, if I do whatever it was that I was doing or I don't do anything at all. How happy will I be in the future? And that gave me all the motivation I needed to set it up.

Vicki Knights, Family Photographer, *www.vickiknights.co.uk*, London, England

You have to believe in your product as well, or service or whatever it is. You need to be able to be 100% behind it. You need to absolutely know that you've got something you're proud of and then your pride and your enthusiasm will come across in whatever conversation you are having.

And the self belief, yes, it gets dented from time to time because you might suddenly have somebody who makes a negative comment and it can really knock you down specially in the early stages. You could kind of give up on everything over one comment and you have to be strong enough really to get beyond that and say to yourself, now hang on, that's one person's opinion, and that's against all these people's opinions who are very positive about this, and you have to keep going.

Helen Wooldridge, Cuddledry,
*www.cuddledry.com,* Somerset, England

For once in my life (because I am one of those people who is always aware of what other people are thinking about me and wondering, am I a decent person? Do they like me?) A switch flipped in me and I decided, you know what, I don't really care what other people think and whether they think that I'm crazy or I'm doing the right thing, I am going to go for this.

Debra McVicker, Hampton Blue,
*www.hamptonblue.co.uk,* Belfast, Northern Ireland

I know that I would not be happy unless I was helping people. I know that that's what I do in life. I know that I want my daughter to grow up with a mum that she sees, you know, is doing things and creating things and helping people. For me, I feel that that gives her a strong role model.

Alli Price, Motivating Mum,
*www.motivatingmum.co.uk*, London, England

If you look at the jobs we do with the children, they're unpaid. We have a team of 20 mums who live around Europe who work for us and who go and visit the properties and who let them on our behalf. They come over here and they do two days of training and then they go and they start charging for their time. And they say to me what about charging for my time? Well, your time is precious, why should anybody have your time for nothing. Your time is valuable, your knowledge is valuable. You've got to believe that and if you don't believe it, if you don't believe in yourself, you can't sell yourself nor your idea. And it is as simple as that really. You somehow got to find a way to be able to make it work for you and believe in yourself.

Wendy Shand, Tots To Travel,
*www.totstotravel.co.uk*, Peterborough, England

If you could see any of my personal reviews that I received when I worked in big corporations, every one of them said 'Melissa does a great job, but she needs to believe in herself more.' Every one, without fail. And my husband will tear his hair out at my lack of self belief. I'm constantly questioning myself, saying 'I don't know if I'm doing a good enough job, I'm sure that at any moment all my clients are going to abandon me because I'm not doing enough for them.' I constantly question myself and doubt myself. It's almost to the point of being ridiculous. And this sailing challenge, I don't know. it was one of those things where I thought 'What the heck, I'm going to go for it.' So I think maybe inherently I am a self-confident person, but in my day to day thing I constantly question myself. And I don't necessarily think that's a bad thing, but I do wish that I was slightly more able to believe in myself on a consistent basis, because that would take little bit of the stress off.

Melissa Talago, PeekaBoo Communications, www.peekaboocoms.co.uk, Berkshire, England (participant in the first leg of the world clipper race from the UK to Brazil, Autumn 2009)

I have done sales throughout my career and the only sales that I've been successful at are things I believe in. Whether it's for a charity fund raising or recruitment or whatever and the reason worked is because I believe people saw that and that's why they bought the idea from me.

Naz Lewis, Back2work Mum, *www.back2workmum.co.uk*, Surrey, England

I remember when Alice was born (she's my first child) I had a full time member of staff but she's a single mother and her son contracted measles so consequently she couldn't come in and run the shop for me. Alice was a week old and so I had to come in with Alice and answer telephone calls while she was breast feeding. I obviously got into a bit of a spin with burning the candles at both ends and it really wasn't a very pleasant place to be in. Initially with my first child, I was really struggling to get that balance. You know, I'd never had a child before and to me, my business was my baby as well.

Karen Simmonds, Travel Matters,
*www.travelmatters.co.uk*, London, England

---

It is a big risk. You're taking a huge leap into the unknown aren't you? I know, most of my friends I speak to, even when I was trying to set up I think a lot of them thought I was absolutely crazy doing it. You know, how are you going to afford this? How are you going to go about this? And what if it doesn't work? It's like you don't even think about it isn't going to work. It's going to work and you know what, if it doesn't work, I'll do something else. When I was younger I always had ideas and I never did anything so when this one came up, it was kind of I have to do this because I've watched so many of my ideas come and go with other people doing exactly what I thought of. So this time around, I said no, I am going to do this. I think that was my driving force.

Jill Barker, Green Baby,
*www.greenbaby.co.uk*, London, England

I do think we're lucky to have been born into these times really when women are at work and there are so many inspirational women who have proven that it is possible to reach to the top of their profession whilst bringing up a family. And I think people need to adopt the idea that right, if they can do it I can do it and if you make the right size steps for you then you're less likely to get knocked back.

Karen Sherr, Musical Minis,
*www.musicalminis.co.uk*, Middlesex, England

I have to say that after the initial period of birth when my kids first came along I never felt as creative, as passionate, as motivated in my whole entire life. You know, having my babies, it really created an absolute fire within me really about doing something for myself but that also involved being a parent, enabled me to be at home with them, feel close to them but also at the same time enabled me to realise a few dreams that were inspired, by having children.

Monic Joint, Mummy Must Have,
*www.mummymusthave.com*, Southampton, England

I guess my one piece of advice to mums lacking in self-belief is to remember that feeling, after you gave birth, when you looked at the little bundle in your arms and thought I created this! After the pain you went through during the delivery, surely, if you can go through that, you can do anything!

Karen Muxworthy, *www.karenmuxworthy.com*,
Freedom Events, *www.freedomevents-sussex.com*

Self belief is absolutely key. One of the things about self belief is that it has to come from inside. The self is really important. However much people tell you you're doing a good job and you are great unless you believe it inside, it doesn't mean anything. Actually, if you can believe it inside, then it doesn't matter what other people say about you either because you believe it.

And I feel very grateful the idea of *Bravissimo* came when it did and I was able to do what I did. I was able to be a hands-on mum at home and set up a business.

You can do the things that you want to do in your life whilst still being a good mum. It is hard. We are expected to do everything. We're expected to be, (as you say,) successful in business, fantastic parents, and always have beautiful tidy houses and home cooked meals and all kinds of things. I think probably, I like most people, muddle through. Do some bits OK and fail at other bits. You know, we're all human aren't we and I think that a good thing to know as well, is that you're not perfect but you do your best.

I think you've got to have self belief and a belief that you know what's best. That's really one of the real markers of an entrepreneur. It's very important.

Sarah Tremellen, Bravissimo,<br>
*www.bravissimo.com*, Leamington Spa, England

## Case Study

### From Child Minder to Mumpreneur

But I have no simple ideas and I'm not passionate about anything other than I want to work from home and I love my children. What can I do?

Well what about childminding? It's the most common form of business that mums follow. Would it suit you?

Check out our real mum case study on the following pages...

In 1997, my little boy got himself a baby sister. I remember the health visitor saying: Now you've got two children I suppose you'll be giving up your usual line of work and taking up childminding from home!

Definitely not was my response... That role takes a certain kind of person, and I don't think I'm it!

Soon after I provisionally booked two separate childminders, as I couldn't find one with two vacancies, I also calculated that my take-home pay, in real terms, would not be making any vast contribution to the household income once the childcare costs and the general cost of working were deducted. Frankly, there were claimants who signed on at my office who'd be getting a bigger pay packet than I was! There had to be some other way...That was the moment I remembered the words of the health visitor and thought that perhaps she had something there.

It was exciting and scary at the same time. Me? Self employed? Who'd have thought? But then there were the niggling doubts... What if I didn't get the work?

What if I didn't bond with other people's children? What if I didn't see eye to eye with the parents?

Simon had his reservations, too, but was very supportive. After much discussion and a lot of soul searching, I decided to take the plunge. At the time, it was probably one of the biggest risks I had ever taken. I was leaving behind the security of a permanent job and a career that had stability, familiarity and a pension.

I was very lucky and landed on my feet pretty quickly, thanks to the childminder network I'd discovered in my area. There was a local co-ordinator who would put parents in touch with childminders with vacancies, so, after meetings with several prospective clients, vacancy number one was soon filled by a 10 month old baby boy, who could happily join my little girl in my second-hand double buggy!

Very early on I took advantage of a council-run, evening training course, covering things like child protection, contract wording, record-keeping & behaviour management. It was good to learn ways of tightening up on knowledge and practices already in place. The best bit for me was that, most of the time, childminding didn't really feel like work – it was as if my children had their friends over every day! The chores of feeding and nappy changing were an extension of what I was already doing anyway, although a few years later, when my youngest was long out of nappies, I did find one particular child's regular nappy contents rather stomach-churning!

About 7 months after my youngest started school, I developed a terrible back strain, brought on by repeatedly lifting a 6 month old baby in and out of my people carrier vehicle in his 'carry-tot' car seat. Despite medication and physiotherapy I could soon see my back wasn't going to get better if I continued to childmind.

During my five years of childminding I decided it was also important to keep in touch with the adult world, and soon after my eldest started primary school, I became an active member of the school's Parent Teacher Association, organising fund-raising events like fashion shows, Christmas fairs, quiz nights, parties and one year, a huge auction of promises that was so successful it's still talked about nearly a decade later. PTA work kept me busy, and there were often times when my childminding day ended and my PTA evening started, but it was a fun way to keep my brain active and utilise my excellent organisational skills. During this time I also began to dabble in web design. With this new found expertise, I was soon commissioned to develop a site for the school's PTA, and it was a great new way to share news and promote fundraising events.

I was no longer limited to being at home for my children as they were both in full time primary school so it really was time to move on. Childminding had been a great way of earning a living whilst still being around for my kids, but continuing wasn't an option.

I very quickly managed to find myself a part-time, term-time only office job in a local education office, which, once again, fitted in quite nicely with domestic circumstances. except, after a time, I did find myself missing the freedom of being my own boss and the thought of self-employment began to beckon once more.

In January 2005, soon after a terrible event in South East Asia, I was approached by a friend I'd worked with on the school PTA to help pull off a 'Grand Tsunami Auction' in the local town. He remembered how I'd single-handedly coordinated the school Auction of Promises and invited me to join the small group of local business people who were joining forces to try and do something to help the victims of the Asian Tsunami. With only three weeks' notice I somehow managed to piece together the ambitious event, pulling in donations of auction items and services, designing the auction programme, scripting the 200+ auction lot descriptions for the auctioneer to read out and devising job descriptions for those involved on the night. To cut a long story short, I'm proud to say the short-notice, one-off event raised over £17K to help rebuild lives in Sri-Lanka, providing new homes and fishing boats for survivors on the tsunami-stricken island. Having given up my PTA work 18 months earlier, that night I realised how much I missed the world of event organising, and for weeks and months later, people I knew were coming up to me saying I should take it up professionally!

In 2006, after organising a huge bash for my 40th birthday, I decided to take the plunge once more, but this time, I worked out that I could start off doing this on a part time basis alongside my term-time job. And so, Freedom Events was born!

In reality my business is still in its infancy, but I'm beginning to build up a client base that can only increase over time, thanks to word of mouth that usually follows a successful event. I'm continuing to be approached by individuals and small businesses requiring websites.

Ultimately, I guess I have a lot to thank childminding for. Not only was it a great way to add to the household income whilst still being around for my kids, but it was also a great introduction to self-employment and it gave me the confidence to take risks and believe in myself. I doubt I would ever have reached the decision to set up in event organising & web design from home had I not had certain experiences thrown my way when I was working with children in my own home.

Karen Muxworthy, *www.karenmuxworthy.com*,
Freedom Events, *www.freedomevents-sussex.com*

# A Mother's Wisdom

We hope you are now believing that you can do this. Being self-employed, running your own business is a wonderful way of balancing work and family life in a way that suits you. It's a great adventure and very rewarding, if hard work. But then staying at home full time or trying to balance motherhood with a traditional job is not easy either.

Before launching into Part Four, where you can play around with your business ideas, some of our wise Mum Ultrapreneurs share a few words about their own mothers, their final thoughts or their personal top tips for being a great Mum Ultrapreneur. Be inspired:

---

I think we've come a long way in the last five years in terms of the Mumpreneur thing. I mean much as we love to hate that phrase. I think when I was beginning to move the idea my friends, in the mums and toddlers group, were probably looking at me in a slightly bemused way. They weren't particularly interested but I think that's because they hadn't really seen it done before. Now it's very much more commonplace for mums to get up and do something and say, you know, I'm going to start a website, I'm going to do this and I'm going to that and then actually do it.

Wendy Shand, Tots To Travel,
*www.totstotravel.co.uk*, Peterborough, England

---

I think everybody should know that they can actually achieve what they want to achieve. In other words you can do anything you like, and I think that would be my tip. You can do it if you want to.

Sarah Sherrington, Illustrator, Sarah Sherrington Designs,
*www.sarahsherrington.co.uk*, London, England

> I definitely wasn't green before I had my son. That's definitely something that came about by having him. Realising how much rubbish I was throwing away I started to worry what kind of planet I was going to leave my kid and what was he going to inherit. We're all making an absolute mess of this place. Our poor children are going to be the ones having to sort it out. I think that's what happens when you become a parent. You become responsible. You think I'm going to start doing something for my kids whereas when you're young and single, you don't even think twice about things, do you?
>
> Jill Barker, Green Baby,
> *www.greenbaby.co.uk*, London, England

> Constantly keep your eyes, your ears and your heart open. Always carry around a notebook with you, keep writing everything down throughout the day. You know, write little messages to yourself to keep yourself going. Evaluate how you're going that day, that week, that month. Keep track of your successes. Keep track of anything you've learnt how to deal with, anything you've learnt that is new. Remember how proud you are in each and every little step that you've overcome every day that goes by. Be proud of that. And keep people around you that are going to keep you feeling enthusiastic. You know, it's powerful and I think if you keep those influences around you, you will always feel like you've got the enthusiasm and drive to be successful.
>
> Monic Joint, Mummy Must Have,
> *www.mummymusthave.com*, Southampton, England

I think it's very, very important for women to realise that this notion that we must be at home for every minute of our children's lives and be physically present is a totally new construction. The reality is that, if you look at the 18th century, the majority of women whether they were mothers or not, were working outside the home or bringing their work in.

At the heart of what I believe is saying to women, you have a choice. If you can afford it you can be at home all the time and if that's what you want to do, that's fine. But my experience really is that when women feel safe, when they know they're not going to be judged, most women will say they would like to do something which would take them out of the home for a certain length of time everyday or have a project that they're working on as well as be with their children.

> Martine Brennan, Contented Living Publishing and Coaching, *www.contentedliving.com* and Author of *Happiness It's Just A Habit, www.happinessitsjustahabit.com*, Co. Kerry, Ireland

It's a really interesting dynamic because I think people think of business and being an entrepreneur as that you have to really hard faced and really goal focused and going for it all the time. But in reality I think you can take it at your own pace and that's the wonder of it for new mums, isn't it? You can take it at your own pace, People will be there to help you. It actually can be a very empowering experience.

> Rita Kobrak, Mums to Italy, *www.mum-and-baby-experience.vpweb.co.uk*, London, England

(My mother said to me once that I was acting like a girl with no options). She ended up doing me a favour that day. I now understand what she meant... Because I started behaving, in time I started behaving like a person with options as opposed to being somebody who was going out into the world thinking this is it. And I think that, certainly for many women, the way they think about themselves, the type of relationships they go into, the opportunities that they turn down or avoid or sabotage inadvertently, some self-filling prophecy, you know all these things that we do, as women? We have really got to stop behaving like we don't have options.

At the end of the day we can now create our own opportunities. That is evident in the number of women who are going out there and going for it. Hell, you don't have to wait for somebody to give you your options, make your own.

Natalie Lue, London, England,
Self Employed Mum (*www.selfemployedmum.co.uk*),
Baggage Reclaim (*www.baggagereclaim.co.uk*),
Bambino Goodies (*www.bambinogoodies.co.uk*),
Nest Goodies (*www.nestgoodies.co.uk*)

---

I went to these Mumpreneur meetings, especially the one where I met Sarah Tremellen. She was so down to earth and I thought – I had always had this picture of these entrepreneurs that they would be made of something completely different. I didn't think that they would be like me. But what I really like about her is that she wasn't this hardnosed business woman. She was a real person and really nice and really down to earth and humble and really talented and everything that I've considered, aspired to in a way. And I found it really encouraging to see that normal people do actually do this as well and succeed.

Birgitte Lydum, Baby Beamers,
*www.babybeamers.com*, London, England

> Someone said 'It's really important to do stuff for free, give stuff away for free.' And I've often felt that I'm getting suckered in a way, people are taking too much from me for free. But it is amazing, if you're willing to give something for free, if you're prepared for absolutely no reason at all to help somebody else out, it will pay back a thousand fold.
>
> Melissa Talago, PeekaBoo Communications, www.peekaboocoms.co.uk, Berkshire, England

> You know what, my parents, especially my mother actually, (would say) you can do anything you put your mind to... I remember when I was about seven and I wanted to be an actress I remember them saying right, then you can be an actress. We sat down and we wrote letters and we addressed them to film studios. We didn't know what we were doing but I felt, even at that young age, as long as you're willing to do something and put something in then you can do whatever you like. I think that very much came from my mum, definitely. She has always, always backed everything that I've done.
>
> Claire Wilson, Send A Thought, *www.sendathought.co.uk*, London, England

> I think what in life is true is that a lot of people have ideas but are quite understandably adverse to the risk because, you know, it's much simpler or safer perhaps to have a normal job, to be employed. Polly and I did, a halfway measure. We both had existing jobs, and we carried on with those jobs and we started *Cuddledry* in our spare time. Then we built it to such a point where we could sit down and talk to each other and say hey right, we are now at a stage where we are ready to take that jump and finish with the day job and work full time on *Cuddledry*, which is exactly what we did.
>
> Helen Wooldridge, Cuddledry, *www.cuddledry.com,* Somerset, England

> I do think that for women setting up they do need to be able to separate, to be disciplined. They do need to separate the work life from the home life. For example when the children were little I use to put the answering machine on when they were in the bath or I was helping them with their homework and then return the calls whilst I was cooking supper.
>
> Karen Sherr, Musical Minis,
> *www.musicalminis.co.uk*, Middlesex, England

> I would say the most important thing would be don't reinvent the wheel. Because, for me, one thing that I'm really passionate about at the moment is there's so many mums in business out there and we're all doing the same thing. Try and make contact with other mums in business who aren't necessarily in your industry, maybe they're in a complementary industry, and ask them to mentor you because they can give you a lot of advice and information which they'd be happy to do. You'll move forward a lot quicker.
>
> Alli Price, Motivating Mum,
> *www.motivatingmum.co.uk*, London, England

> I would say that if a woman had recently had a child or has young children at home, and they really want to do something for themselves they should go for it. Think about it, write it down, plan it, go for it. It's a great and exciting time in your life when your kids are small. We don't have to go back to doing what we were doing before we had children. This could be an exciting time for us to find something that's utterly unique to ourselves... Motherhood is powerful. Use that, use it to define what it means to you.
>
> Monic Joint, Mummy Must Have,
> *www.mummymusthave.com*, Southampton, England

It's a very, very strange thing, I think it's a peculiarly female thing. Men don't do this. They don't sit and analyse themselves and question their abilities. in fact, if anything, they over-believe in themselves. Whereas women say 'I'm not sure if I can do that' and then do a brilliant job. I know that's a gross generalisation and I apologise to all the men out there, One thing that the sailing, for example, has taught me is that I am far more capable than I thought I was. There are so many things that I have had to do on this sailing thing that I thought never would I ever be able to do. Engineering, for example. I know nothing about that. I did a sea survival course this weekend and I'm claustrophobic and the thought of getting in a little, enclosed life raft and being bounced around fills me with dread. But I was made the raft leader And I did it! I did it well I think that's something that all women can take on: don't be afraid of trying, do it because you absolutely will be able to do it, no matter how hard it seems.

Melissa Talago, PeekaBoo Communications,<br>www.peekaboocoms.co.uk, Berkshire, England

I would say the majority of the women I have anything to do with are consciously moving away from the corporate lifestyle and I think that's something to do with having had children. They still want to be successful, they still want to have a sense of identity but they don't need to do it within a masculine world. The only men within my sphere of work are website designers, a couple of people who have stuff to do with the internet. That's not conscious, it's evolved that way. It's not dog eat dog. It's a far more supportive and cooperative way of working.

We can do life how we want to do it. I know my husband and I are very consciously mindful of living our lives to be the best parents we can, to be very hands on. And this business is key to that because it means that our lives aren't controlled by anybody else. I can still pick the children up and I'm there if they're sick, and my husband's going to be joining me in doing that so we can be there as pleasant parents and, hopefully, good role models for our children.

Wendy Shand, Tots To Travel,<br>*www.totstotravel.co.uk*, Peterborough, England

My mother was someone who worked and who had time for her family but never made it feel as if one was kind of outstripping or outshining the other and always managed to get that right balance She was the linchpin in the household.

Anna Hayward, Managing Maternity Ltd,<br>*www.managingmaternity.co.uk*, East Sussex, England

There's a lot about my mum that's great, and she gave me plenty that I can really identify with. She was very gifted at amateur dramatics, and did a lot of performance. She was really good and when she was training me during my childhood in North Wales or helping me learn a part for a production that I was in, she would say to me 'sparkle'. So sparkle was my mum's advice. And the other lovely thing she said to me was: 'I don't really know what you'll end up doing or where you're heading but I know that you'll do it well.'

And I thought well, that's great thing for a parent to say. It's not particularly relevant to running a business but to offer a child that trust in who they are and give them that confidence without pushing them in any particular direction is very empowering.

Jennifer Liston-Smith, Managing Maternity Ltd<br>*www.managingmaternity.co.uk*, Llanelwy, Wales

> One final piece of advice is to savour every moment with your own children. I know it's a cliché but it's so true, and I sound like my own mother when I say that they grow so quickly! Before you know it they're independent and preparing to enter the big wide world in their own right. My children are both secondary school age now and I know it won't be too long before the eldest is off to university. Yet another 'scary' prospect, but I know I'll get through it!
>
> Karen Muxworthy, *www.karenmuxworthy.com*,<br>Freedom Events, *www.freedomevents-sussex.com*

Susan Ödev & Mark Weeks

# Part Four

## The SPARKLES Plan

You have made it. You have read our book to this point and you have been inspired by the incredible stories of ordinary mothers who are running their own businesses. Now you are ready to try this for yourself.

So, where do you start? Remember Gemma? She wrote down everything in her Golden Notebook. Writing down our thoughts in a journal or notebook does three things.

Firstly, it's a record of your ideas so you don't forget them. Remember no idea is too simple, so jot everything down so you don't lose it. Play with your thoughts and your words. Feel excited about them. No idea is too crazy either – after all you are only writing them down in a notebook for yourself; no one else will see. Enjoy it.

Secondly, writing your thoughts down helps you to process them more easily. The act of writing forces your conscious mind to organise your ideas into a structure; even if you are just brainstorming. And the written word is a powerful visual aid which helps your conscious mind to focus better. Better still, draw pictures, cut out images from magazines, collect swatches etc. Whichever way you choose to record your thoughts you are physically doing something with them i.e. taking action. Have fun.

And finally - the act of writing makes your ideas come to life, quite literally. Your subconscious mind will focus on what you focus on. Writing your ideas down clarifies your desires and your subconscious will do everything it can to make those wishes come true. If these ideas exist on paper then they can exist in the real world. How wonderful does that feel?

Great! So let's start as Gemma did.

Maybe you already have a business idea – is it a product or a service?

If you know what you would like to explore further then jump to **Part B** of the action plan that follows. If not, take some time for yourself and work through **Part A** first. Ask friends and family to help you if you get stuck – they know you better than you think.

## Part A: The Big Idea

What do I enjoy doing? (hobbies, crafts, interests)

|   |
|---|
|   |

What am I great at that others find difficult?

|   |
|---|
|   |

Do I have an idea for a product or service?

|   |
|---|
|   |

Have I complained about something recently?

|   |
|---|
|   |

Was I looking for something I couldn't find?

[ ]

Have I experienced bad service or wasted a lot of time or money on something?

[ ]

Did a new and exciting product or service fail to meet my expectations?

[ ]

Does that indicate that there's a need for something new or different? (If you wanted it or needed it others may too)

[ ]

Does that product or service already exist in some form?

[ ]

If yes, how can I make it different? What is my USP (Unique Selling Point)?

[ ]

Have I tried the other products/services available?

[ ]

What did I like or dislike about them?

What was my experience?

How can I do it better?

If the idea is totally new is there a potential market?

How do I know there's a market?

What do people *really* want?

How could I deliver what they want?

Brainstorm all your ideas on the next page and remember: no idea is too crazy!

Have you got an idea yet? Maybe you have more than one. Now ask yourself which of these ideas, if there is more than one, fires you up the most?

If you have one idea ask yourself – how do I feel about this? Am I excited by it?

If you feel excited and fired up then take this idea on to Part B.

# Part B: Making It Happen

# Simplicity

Write down your idea in the simplest of words.

For example, Gemma could have written her idea out like this:

> I am creating a business network where estate agents work together with clients, and other estate agents, to sell houses quickly and with minimum stress.

So, simplify your idea here.

|   |
|---|
|   |

Now think about the systems needed to make this work.

What do you think you need to do? Keep it simple. (e.g. set up a website, register my company name, create a prototype, inquire about funding, source potential suppliers, check out the competition, do some market research etc.)

|   |
|---|
|   |

What resources do I need?

|   |
|---|
|   |

Who needs to be involved?

|   |
|---|
|   |

Where can I get support or advice?

How can I test out my idea?

Now draft your To Do List – a plan of action...

## Review Your To Do List

Review your To Do list. Is there an easier way to do any of the things on your list?

For example, you may have put down *market research*: find ways to do it simply and cheaply i.e. using the internet.

Now, look at your idea again. Create an image in your mind of how it will look. Does it appear complex and impossible? Then rethink it. Keep it simple, sexy. Take it back down to basics.

The aim is to have a clear, simple picture of your business idea in your mind so you can describe it easily to yourself and others.

When you are ready, write a short description of your business **here**.

Use these questions to help you:

- What is your product/service?
- What are your key values?
- Where is your market?
- Who are your customers?
- What do they want?
- How do they want it?
- Where do they want it?
- When do they want it?
- How will you reach them?

**Very Important:** Put the idea to one side and let it be for a few days before moving on.

## Passion

OK, now you have explored your simple idea and your concept should be getting clear and easier to describe. Now is this something you want to do for the next five, ten or twenty years?

How does this business idea make you feel?

|  |
|--|
|  |

Since you wrote it down, how many times have you found yourself thinking about it?

- ❏ All the time
- ❏ Quite a lot
- ❏ Once or twice
- ❏ Never

If you answered **Never** – then no matter how good the idea may seem on paper it possibly isn't the right business for you.

Remember: a successful business is a commitment, like having a child. You need to fall in love with it. It *must* be something that makes you excited. It is going to be hard work and you may have to work long hours and make sacrifices.

If you answered that you think about it **all the time** then move on. If you answered **occasionally** or **once or twice** go back to your idea and play with it a bit more. Have fun with it and see if your passion grows. Then when you are ready, move on to **Action**.

## Action

Go back to your To Do list.

It's probably quite long. Look at your list and identify the tasks that need to be done first.

For example, if you have identified that your business will be mostly conducted online then you will probably have *Register your domain name* on your To Do list. This is important but should be done after you have decided on your company name. And deciding on the company name should come after you have researched the market and asked for advice on branding and Search Engine Optimisation (SEO); and if you don't know what that means you probably should research that first!

Then rank the tasks in priority order from 1 to 10.

Now, time is limited as a working mum so the next step is to be honest about how long things will take and when you can find the time to do it. Identify slots of time you can give to the business and then allocate tasks to each slot.

**Important:** You have to do those things during those times! (fingers crossed)

Most books will tell you that you have to perform these tasks during the time specified without fail. We know that sometimes you will be unable to do this because childcare falls through, the baby is sick or you're too tired after a sleepless night. But when things don't go to plan the most important thing is not to beat yourself up but to keep moving down the list whenever you *do* have time. Keep going.

Take action, repeatedly. One small step at a time is fine but keep walking in the right direction.

Stop planning and start doing.

## Relationships

Once you have taken your first few steps you will probably find that, for all your answers, you now have even more questions; that every task you completed created another 10 tasks to do. That's great. It means things are happening and you are on your way.

But remember you may be in business for yourself, but you are not on your own. Take a moment to write names against the following questions.

Who can I rely on in a crisis?

Who makes me feel good about myself?

Who can I be totally myself with?

Who can I talk to if worried?

Who really makes me stop and think about what I am doing?

Who is lively to be with?

Who makes me laugh?

Who introduces me to new ideas, new interests, new people?

Who has a calming effect?

Who understands my situation?

Who has expert knowledge?

Who has done this, or something similar, before?

Who thinks I'm wonderful?

Review this list and see where you may have gaps. Then work out where and how can you fill those gaps i.e. through forums, networking, professional organisations, mother & toddler groups, Twitter?

Do any names appear more than once? Cherish those relationships they will be invaluable.

Now, look at your To Do list – how can these people help you? Ask them!

## Knowing

OK, you have been running with this business idea for a while now. You have explored the concept, tested the market, started to take action etc.

What is your gut telling you?

```
                                              
                                              
```

- Do you feel confident?
- Do you feel excited?
- Are you enjoying the process?
- Are there any niggling doubts?
- Are you worried about other people's reactions?
- Do you feel sure that this is what you want to do?

Listen to your inner voice that comes from your heart not your head.

Find time each day for yourself and sit quietly.

Clear your mind, breathe deeply and relax.

Take action based on what feels right. Small things at first. Practice makes perfect.

# Learning

On your To Do list there may have been a number of tasks you knew you had to do but didn't know how.

Go back and review them. Is there anyone you know who may have the answer? If so ask them.

Be prepared to do a lot of learning and see what you can access for free.

Ask your local Business Link and/or your local Chamber of Commerce for advice and free courses:

- Business Link in England (*www.businesslink.gov.uk*)
- Business Gateway and Highlands and Islands Enterprise in Scotland (*www.bgateway.com* or *www.hie.co.uk*)
- Business Eye in Wales (*www.businesseye.org.uk*)
- Invest Northern Ireland in, you guessed it, Northern Ireland (*www.investni.com*)
- County & City Enterprise Boards in the Republic of Ireland (*www.enterpriseboards.ie*) where you can take free or very cheap courses on all the key subjects.

Check out your local library for books, leaflets and workshops in your area.

Go online and search for free resources and guides.

Hunt out business women networks either on the web or locally.

Ask other Mumpreneurs, attend lunches, conferences etc.

Ask about and attend or, better still, exhibit at relevant trade shows – you'll be amazed at the contacts you find and what you can pick up there from other businesses in your field.

Ask your Bank for free advice.

Talk to the Tax Office and make sure you know what account information you need to keep and what you have to do to register as self employed or as a small business. They are human too and will help you.

Don't forget to read often:

- About other people who have succeeded in business.
- About famous mums and how they cope with work and family life.
- Empowering self help books and magazine articles.

And use the internet. Follow working mum blogs, Twitter with like-minded women and join online forums. Everything can be an opportunity to learn. Grab it! Love it!

## Enthusiasm

Every day before you go to sleep take 10 minutes to reflect on your achievements.

Notice what you have done today.

Write it down in your notebook.

Tick off items on your To Do List.

Record encouraging feedback you have received from family, friends and best of all satisfied customers.

Note down any new ideas.

How did you feel today?

|   |
|---|
|   |

What did you enjoy?

|   |
|---|
|   |

What was good about today?

|  |
|--|
|  |

What do you want more of tomorrow?

|  |
|--|
|  |

Every week look back over everything you have written during these night time reflections.

Award yourself a little treat for all your good work. Something just for you (and maybe the kids sometimes).

Celebrate goals achieved and customers or contracts won.

When your business hits certain milestones like selling the first 10 widgets or the website receives 1000 hits share this news with all those who helped and supported you.

And start planning your business's first birthday party. Remember, just as surviving the first year as a mother means you can do anything this is just the same – so celebrate in style!

## Self-belief

It is vitally important that you stay positive and do everything you can to improve your self-esteem.

Take a few moments now to do the following exercise and repeat it regularly in the future...

Look at yourself in the mirror and repeat the following statements.

- I am a strong, capable woman.
- I am a wonderful mother.
- I am a confident business woman.
- I am creative, talented and resourceful.
- I am naturally resilient.
- I am a great organiser.
- I am awesome at juggling priorities and managing my time.
- I am amazing at sales and promotion.
- I am in control of my finances and my life.
- I am surrounded by supportive friends and family.
- I love, I am loved, I am love.
- I am ME and I SPARKLE.

Say them with pride and lots of energy. Know that they are true. No matter what negative self talk you are having to shout down. The more you do this the quieter those voices will become. So do this as often as you feel you need to. Once a day, once a week, once every hour.

And if you struggle to believe it – act as if you know these statements are facts. Plain and simple facts. Because they are.

# Well Done!

You are well on your way to creating a business life that SPARKLES.

Unless of course you are one of those that have skipped through to the back pages to find out the ending, that is.

If you raced to the back then you have missed our blueprint for running your own business and balancing your family life.

You would have skipped our fictional story of Gemma as she grows her family, grows her business and grows stronger. Which would be a shame because through it we learnt how to live a life that SPARKLES.

Also you wouldn't have read the inspiring words of our entrepreneurial mums; showing that yes, sometimes life can be tough but, with a little persistence, purpose and passion you can achieve your goals.

But most of all you wouldn't now be able to use our SPARKLES plan to generate and develop an amazing business idea that you can now build alongside your family commitments.

So go back, read again and again, dip in and out and when you're ready.

Go on, go for it!

There is a list of suggested further reading at the back of this book and on the website (*www.mum-ultrapreneur.com*) there are links where you will find even more advice and support.

Visit *www.mum-ultrapreneur.com/bonuses* and listen to our female entrepreneurs talk candidly about their family and business lives.

Sign up for our newsletter and keep up to date with lots of exciting news and offers that will help you live a business life that SPARKLES.

And let us know how you get on. Maybe we'll feature you in our next book!

Keep in touch and keep sparkling!

**Susan & Mark**
*www.mum-ultrapreneur.com*

Susan Ödev & Mark Weeks

# Mum Ultrapreneur Reading List

Gemma read a lot of books and, as you can probably tell, so did we! Here is a list of the books mentioned in Mum Ultrapreneur to guide, advise, support and inspire you.

| Title | Author | Publisher | ISBN |
|---|---|---|---|
| **Self Help and books on the Law of Attraction** | | | |
| *The Secret* | Rhonda Byrne | Atria Books | 1582701709 |
| *Excuse me, Your Life is Waiting: The astonishing power of feelings* | Lynn Grabhorn | Hampton Road Publishing | 1571743812 |
| *End the struggle and dance with life: How to build yourself up when the world gets you down* | Susan Jeffers | St. Martins Griffin | 0312155220 |
| *Think and Grow Rich* | Napoleon Hill | Wilder | 1604591870 |
| *The 80/20 Principle: The secret of achieving more with less* | Richard Koch | Broadway Business | 0385491743 |
| *The Street Kids Guide To Having it all: A practical and spiritual approach to living the life of your dreams* | John Assaraf | OneCoach Inc | 0972621423 |
| *Excuse Me, Your Life is Now: Mastering the law of attraction* | Doreen Banaszak | Hampton Roads Publishing | 1571745432 |

| | | | |
|---|---|---|---|
| *Feel the fear and do it anyway* | Susan Jeffers | Ballatine Books | 0345487427 |

## Business Books

| | | | |
|---|---|---|---|
| P.U.S.H. For Success, | Saira Khan | Vermilion | 0091910447 |
| *Leadership (Tom Peters Essentials)* | Thomas .J. Peters | DK Adult | 0756610559 |
| *Selling is a women's game: Fifteen powerful reasons why women outsell men* | Nicki Joy & Susan Kane-Benson | Harper Paperbacks | 038077416X |
| Business as Unusual: My entrepreneurial journey – Profits with principles | Anita Roddick | Anita Roddick Books | 0954395956 |
| Business Nightmares: When entrepreneurs hit crisis point | Rachel Elnaugh | Crimson Publishing | 185458474X |
| *Start your business week by week: How to plan & launch your successful business one step at a time* | Steve Parks | Prentice Hall Business Publishing | 273694472 |

## Other highly recommended books to motivate and inspire

| | | | |
|---|---|---|---|
| *The Mumpreneur Guide: Start your own business* | Antonia Chitty, Emma Cooper and Jess Williams | Ac Pr | 955534526 |

| | | | |
|---|---|---|---|
| *Secrets of successful women entrepreneurs: How ten leading business women turned a good idea into a fortune* | Sue Stockdale | Bookshaker | 1905430035 |
| *Inspiring women: 25 top female entrepreneurs reveal how real women succeed in business* | Michelle Rosenberg | Crimson Publishing | 1854584106 |
| *Making it: Women entrepreneurs reveal their secrets of success.* | Lou Grimson | Capstone | 1841127000 |
| *Super Mummy: The ultimate mumpreneur's guide to online business success* | Mel McGee | Bookshaker | 1905430515 |
| *Kitchen Table Tycoon* | Anita Naik | Piakus Books | 0749927917 |
| *Make it your business: the ultimate business start up guide for women* | Bella Mehta & Lucy Martin | How to Books | 1905862008 |
| *Spare room start up: How to start a business from home* | Emma Jones | Harriman House Publishers | 1905641680 |
| *In good company: the essential business start up guide for women* | Rebecca Jordan & Kirsty Weir | A + C Black Publishers | 0713676264 |
| **And for fun** | | | |
| *The Mumpreneur Diaries: Business, Babies or Bust – One mother of a year* | Mosey Jones | Collins | 000729878X |

Susan Ödev & Mark Weeks

# References

P.U.S.H. For Success, Saira Khan, Vermilion ISBN 009191044-7

Check Out *The Secret* By Rhonda Byrne or Susan's favourite: *Excuse Me Your Life Is Waiting,* By Lynn Grabhorn

*Tom Peters Essentials: Leadership,* Thomas J. Peters

*Ask And It Is Given – Abraham-Hicks or The Secret,* Rhonda Byrne

*Business As Usual,* Anita Roddick

*End The Struggle And Dance With Life,* Susan Jeffers

*Think And Grow Rich,* Napoleon Hill

*A Spoonful Of Sugar,* (Song) from Walt Disney's Mary Poppins

S = Specific, M = Measurable, A = Achievable Or Agreeable, R = Realistic Or Resourced, T = Time Bound

*The 80/20 Principle: The Secret Of Achieving More With Less,* Richard Koch

Similarities To Doris Lessing's *Golden Notebook* are purely intentional!

*The street kid's guide to having it all. - a practical approach for designing and living the life of your dreams,* John Assaraf

*We're Going On A Bear Hunt,* Michael Rosen And Helen Oxenbury

*Excuse Me Your Life Is Now,* Doreen Banaszak

*The New Testament And Psalms – No 23,* The Gideons International

*Let It Be,* (Song) Lennon And McCartney

*Just William Stories,* Richmal Crompton

# SECRETS OF SUCCESSFUL WOMEN ENTREPRENEURS

## HOW TEN LEADING BUSINESS WOMEN TURNED A GOOD IDEA INTO A FORTUNE

linda bennett   glenda stone   geetie singh   penny streeter   josephine carpenter

michelle mone   yvonne thompson   helen swaby   marilyn orcharton   julie meyer

## SUE STOCKDALE

# the Virtual Assistant handbook

insider secrets for
starting and running your
own profitable VA business

Nadine Hill

**com**

www.ingramcontent.com/pod-product-compliance
Lightning Source LLC
Chambersburg PA
CBHW060504090426
42735CB00011B/2111